TEACH YOURSELF
INTERNET &
WORLD WIDE WEB
VISUALLY

IDG's **3-D Visual** Series

From
maranGraphics

IDG Books Worldwide, Inc.
An International Data Group Company
Foster City, CA • Indianapolis • Chicago • Dallas

Teach Yourself Internet & World Wide Web Visually

Published by
IDG Books Worldwide, Inc.
An International Data Group Company
919 E. Hillsdale Blvd., Suite 400
Foster City, CA 94404

Library of Congress Catalog Card No.:
ISBN: 0-7645-6020-4

Printed in the United States of America
10 9 8 7 6 5 4 3 2 1

XX/XX/XX/XX/XX

Distributed in the United States by IDG Books Worldwide, Inc.

Distributed by Transworld Publishers Limited in the United Kingdom and Europe; by WoodsLane Pty. Ltd. for Australia; by WoodsLane Enterprises Ltd. for New Zealand; by Longman Singapore Publishers Ltd. for Singapore, Malaysia, Thailand, and Indonesia; by Simron Pty. Ltd. for South Africa; by Toppan Company Ltd. for Japan; by Distribuidora Cuspide for Argentina; by Livraria Cultura for Brazil; by Ediciencia S.A. for Ecuador; by Addison-Wesley Publishing Company for Korea; by Ediciones ZETA S.C.R. Ltda. for Peru; by WS Computer Publishing Company, Inc., for the Philippines; by Unalis Corporation for Taiwan; by Contemporanea de Ediciones for Venezuela. Authorized Sales Agent: Anthony Rudkin Associates for the Middle East and North Africa.

For corporate orders, please call maranGraphics at 800-469-6616.
For general information on IDG Books Worldwide's books in the U.S., please call our Consumer Customer Service department at 800-762-2974.
For reseller information, including discounts and premium sales, please call our Reseller Customer Service department at 800-434-3422.
For information on where to purchase IDG Books Worldwide's books outside the U.S., please contact our International Sales department at 415-655-3023 or fax 415-655-3299.
For information on foreign language translations, please contact our Foreign & Subsidiary Rights department at 415-655-3021 or fax 415-655-3281.
For sales inquiries and special prices for bulk quantities, please contact our Sales department at 415-655-3200.
For information on using IDG Books Worldwide's books in the classroom or for ordering examination copies, please contact our Educational Sales department at 800-434-2086 or fax 817-251-8174.
For press review copies, author interviews, or other publicity information, please contact our Public Relations department at 415-655-3000 or fax 415-655-3299.
For authorization to photocopy items for corporate, personal, or educational use, please contact maranGraphics at 800-469-6616.

Trademark Acknowledgments

© 1997
maranGraphics, Inc.

The 3-D illustrations are the copyright of maranGraphics, Inc.

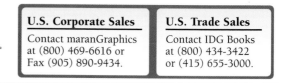

U.S. Corporate Sales	**U.S. Trade Sales**
Contact maranGraphics at (800) 469-6616 or Fax (905) 890-9434.	Contact IDG Books at (800) 434-3422 or (415) 655-3000.

Welcome to the world of IDG Books Worldwide.

IDG Books Worldwide, Inc., is a subsidiary of International Data Group, the world's largest publisher of computer-related information and the leading global provider of information services on information technology. IDG was founded more than 25 years ago and now employs more than 8,500 people worldwide. IDG publishes more than 270 computer publications in over 75 countries (see listing below). More than 90 million people read one or more IDG publications each month.

Launched in 1990, IDG Books Worldwide is today the #1 publisher of best-selling computer books in the United States. We are proud to have received eight awards from the Computer Press Association in recognition of editorial excellence and three from Computer Currents' First Annual Readers' Choice Awards. Our best-selling ...For Dummies® series has more than 25 million copies in print with translations in 30 languages. IDG Books Worldwide, through a joint venture with IDG's Hi-Tech Beijing, became the first U.S. publisher to publish a computer book in the People's Republic of China. In record time, IDG Books Worldwide has become the first choice for millions of readers around the world who want to learn how to better manage their businesses.

Our mission is simple: Every one of our books is designed to bring extra value and skill-building instructions to the reader. Our books are written by experts who understand and care about our readers. The knowledge base of our editorial staff comes from years of experience in publishing, education, and journalism - experience which we use to produce books for the '90s. In short, we care about books, so we attract the best people. We devote special attention to details such as audience, interior design, use of icons, and illustrations. And because we use an efficient process of authoring, editing, and desktop publishing our books electronically, we can spend more time ensuring superior content and spend less time on the technicalities of making books.

You can count on our commitment to deliver high-quality books at competitive prices on topics you want to read about. At IDG Books Worldwide, we continue in the IDG tradition of delivering quality for more than 25 years. You'll find no better book on a subject than one from IDG Books Worldwide.

John Kilcullen
President and CEO
IDG Books Worldwide, Inc.

IDG Books Worldwide, Inc., is a subsidiary of International Data Group, the world's largest publisher of computer-related information and the leading global provider of information services on information technology. International Data Group publishes over 276 computer publications in over 75 countries. Ninety million people read one or more International Data Group publications each month. International Data Group's publications include: Argentina: Annuario de Informatica, Computerworld Argentina, PC World Argentina; Australia: Australian Macworld, Client/Server Journal, Computer Living, Computerworld, Computerworld 100, Digital News, IT Casebook, Network World, On-line World Australia, PC World, Publishing Essentials, Reseller, WebMaster; Austria: Computerwelt Osterreich, Networks Austria, PC Tip; Belarus: PC World Belarus; Belgium: Data News; Brazil: Annuário de Informática, Computerworld Brazil, Connections, Super Game Power, Macworld, PC Player, PC World Brazil, Publish Brazil, Reseller News; Bulgaria: Computerworld Bulgaria, Networkworld/Bulgaria, PC & MacWorld Bulgaria; Canada: CIO Canada, Client/Server World, ComputerWorld Canada, InfoCanada, Network World Canada; Chile: Computerworld Chile, PC World Chile; Colombia: Computerworld Colombia, PC World Colombia; Costa Rica: PC World Centro America; The Czech and Slovak Republics: Computerworld Czechoslovakia, Elektronika Czechoslovakia, Macworld Czech Republic, PC World Czechoslovakia; Denmark: Communications World, Computerworld Danmark, Macworld Danmark, PC Privat Danmark, PC World Danmark, PC World Danmark Supplements, TECH World; Dominican Republic: PC World Republica Dominicana; Ecuador: PC World Ecuador; Egypt: Computerworld Middle East, PC World Middle East; El Salvador: PC World Centro America; Finland: MikroPC, Tietoverkko, Tietoviikko; France: Distributique, Golden, Hebdo-Distributique, Info PC, Le Guide du Monde Informatique, Le Monde Informatique, Reseaux & Telecoms; Germany: Computer Partner, Computerwoche, Computerwoche Extra, Computerwoche Focus, I/M Information Management, Macwelt, PC Welt; Greece: GamePro, Multimedia World; Guatemala: PC World Centro America; Honduras: PC World Centro America; Hong Kong: Computerworld Hong Kong, PCWorld Hong Kong, Publish in Asia; Hungary: ABCD CD-ROM, Computerworld Szamitastechnika, PC & Mac World Hungary, PC-X Magazine; Iceland: Tolvuheimur/PC World Island; India: Information Systems Computerworld, PC World India, Publish in Asia; Indonesia: InfoKomputer PC World, Komputek Computerworld, Publish in Asia; Ireland: ComputerScope, PC Live!; Israel: People & Computers; Italy: Computerworld Italia, Computerworld Italia Special Editions, Macworld Italia, Networking Italia, PC Shopping, PC World Italia, PC World/Walt Disney; Japan: DTP World, HP Open World Japan, Macworld Japan, Nikkei Personal Computing, Open World Japan, OS/2 World Japan, SunWorld Japan, Windows World Japan; Kenya: East African Computer News; Korea: Hi-Tech Information/Computerworld, Macworld Korea, PC World Korea; Macedonia: PC World Macedonia; Malaysia: Computerworld Malaysia, PC World Malaysia, Publish in Asia; Mexico: Computerworld Mexico, Macworld, PC World Mexico; Myanmar: PC World Myanmar; Netherlands: Computer! Totaal, LAN Magazine, LanWorld Buyers Guide, Macworld, Net Magazine, Totaal! Beurskrant; New Zealand: Absolute Beginner's Guide, Computer Buyer, Computer Industry Directory, Computerworld New Zealand, MTB, Network World, PC World New Zealand; Nicaragua: PC World Centro America; Nigeria: PC World Nigeria; Norway: Computerworld Norge, Computerworld Hong Kong, (Datamagasinet), CW Rapport Norge, IDG's KURSGUIDE, Macworld Norge, Multimediaworld, PC World Ekspress, PC World Nettverk, PC World Norge, PC World's Produktguide, Windows World Spesial; Pakistan: Computerworld Pakistan, PC World Pakistan; Panama: PC World Panama; P. R. of China: China Computer Users, China Computerworld, China Infoworld, China Telecom World Weekly, Computer & Communication, Electronic Design China, Electronics Today, Electronics Weekly, Game Camp, Game Soft, Network World China, PC World China, Popular Computer Weekly, Software Weekly, Software World, Telecom World; Peru: Computerworld Peru, PC World Profesional Peru, PC World Peru; Poland: Computerworld Poland, Computerworld Special Report, Macworld, Networld, PC World Komputer; Philippines: Computerworld Philippines, PC World Philippines, Publish in Asia; Portugal: Cerebro/PC World, Computerworld/Correio Informático, Dealer World Portugal, Mac*In/PC*In, Multimedia World Portugal; Puerto Rico: PC World Puerto Rico; Romania: Computerworld Romania, PC World Romania, Telecom Romania; Russia: Computerworld Russia, Mir PK, Sety; Singapore: Computerworld Singapore, PC World Singapore, Publish in Asia; Slovenia: MONITOR; South Africa: Computing S.A., InfoWorld S.A., Network World S.A., Software World; Spain: Computerworld Espa-a, COMUNICACIONES WORLD, Dealer World, Macworld Espa-a, PC World Espa-a; Sweden: CAP&Design, Computer Sweden, Corporate Computing, MacWorld, Maxi Data, MikroDatorn, Nätverk & Kommunikation, PC/Aktiv, PC World, Windows World; Switzerland: Computerworld Schweiz, Macworld Schweiz, PCtip; Taiwan: Computerworld Taiwan, Macworld Taiwan, PC World Taiwan, Publish Taiwan, Windows World; Thailand: Thai Computerworld, Publish in Asia; Turkey: Computerworld Turkiye, MACWORLD Turkiye, PC WORLD Turkiye; Ukraine: Computerworld Kiev, Computers & Software, Multimedia World Ukraine, PC World Ukraine; United Kingdom: Acorn User, Amiga Action, Amiga Computing, Appletalk, Computing, GamePro, Macworld, Network News, Parents and Computers, PC Advisor, PC Home, PSX Pro UK, The WEB; United States: Cable in the Classroom, CD Review, CIO Magazine, Computerworld, Computerworld Client/Server Journal, Digital Video Magazine, DOS World, Federal Computer Week, GamePro, InfoWorld, I-Way, JavaWorld, Macworld, Multimedia World, Netscape World Online, Network World, PC Entertainment, PC World, Publish, SunWorld Online, SWATPro Magazine, Video Event, WebMaster; Uruguay: PC World Uruguay; Venezuela: Computerworld Venezuela, PC World Venezuela; and Vietnam: PC World Vietnam.

Every maranGraphics book represents
the extraordinary vision and commitment of a unique family:
the Maran family of Toronto, Canada.

Back Row (from left to right): *Sherry Maran, Rob Maran, Richard Maran, Maxine Maran, Jill Maran.*

Front Row (from left to right): *Judy Maran, Ruth Maran.*

Richard Maran is the company founder and its inspirational leader. He developed maranGraphics' proprietary communication technology called "visual grammar." This book is built on that technology—empowering readers with the easiest and quickest way to learn about computers.

Ruth Maran is the Author and Architect—a role Richard established that now bears Ruth's distinctive touch. She creates the words and visual structure that are the basis for the books.

Judy Maran is the Project Coordinator. She works with Ruth, Richard and the highly talented maranGraphics illustrators, designers and editors to transform Ruth's material into its final form.

Rob Maran is the Technical and Production Specialist. He makes sure the state-of-the-art technology used to create these books always performs as it should.

Sherry Maran manages the Reception, Order Desk and any number of areas that require immediate attention and a helping hand.

Jill Maran is a jack-of-all-trades and dynamo who fills in anywhere she's needed anytime she's back from university.

Maxine Maran is the Business Manager and family sage. She maintains order in the business and family—and keeps everything running smoothly.

CREDITS

Author & Architect:
Paul Whitehead
Ruth Maran

Copy & Development Editor:
Kelleigh Wing

Project Coordinator:
Judy Maran

Editor:
Brad Hilderley

Proofreaders:
Wanda Lawrie
Peter Lejcar
Tina Veltri
Carol Barclay

Layout Designer:
Christie Van Duin

Illustrations & Screens:
Tamara Poliquin
Chris K.C. Leung
Russell C. Marini
Ben Lee
Jeff Jones
Jamie Bell

Indexer:
Kelleigh Wing

Post Production:
Robert Maran

ACKNOWLEDGMENTS

Thanks to the dedicated staff of maranGraphics, including Carol Barclay, Jamie Bell, Francisco Ferreira, Brad Hilderley, Jeff Jones, Wanda Lawrie, Ben Lee, Peter Lejcar, Chris K.C. Leung, Michael W. MacDonald, Jill Maran, Judy Maran, Maxine Maran, Robert Maran, Sherry Maran, Russell C. Marini, Tamara Poliquin, Christie Van Duin, Tina Veltri, Paul Whitehead and Kelleigh Wing.

Finally, to Richard Maran who originated the easy-to-use graphic format of this guide. Thank you for your inspiration and guidance.

SCREEN SHOT PERMISSIONS

The Internet & World Wide Web

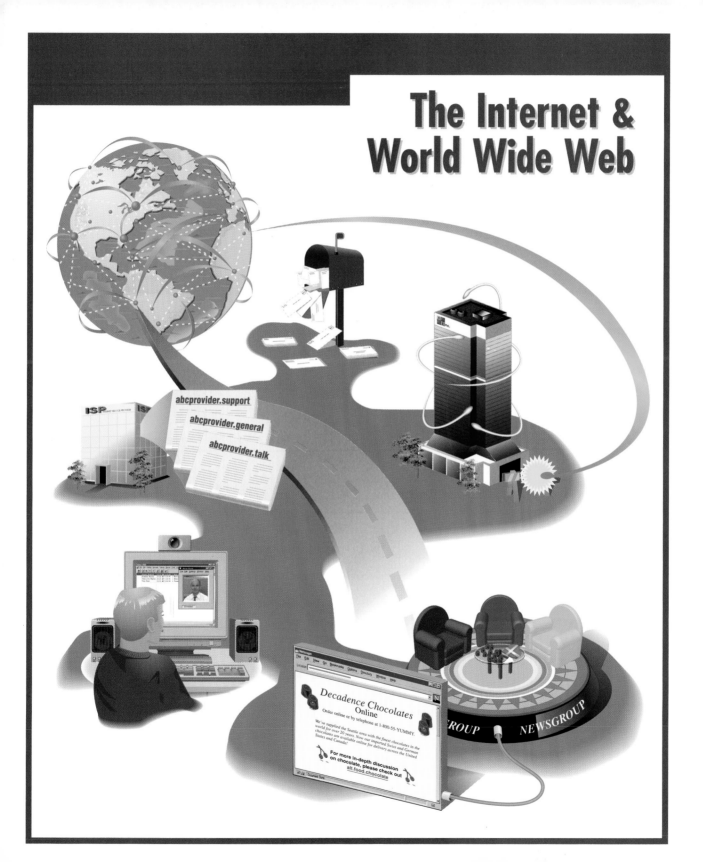

TABLE OF CONTENTS

THE INTERNET

1

CONNECT TO THE INTERNET

2

INFORMATION AVAILABLE ON THE INTERNET

3

THE WORLD WIDE WEB

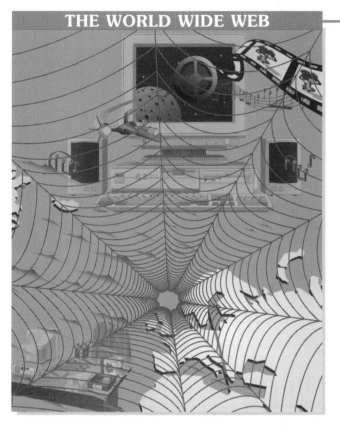

SEARCH THE WORLD WIDE WEB

TABLE OF CONTENTS

CREATE WEB PAGES

ELECTRONIC MAIL

MAILING LISTS

NEWSGROUPS

CHAT

TABLE OF CONTENTS

TELNET — 11

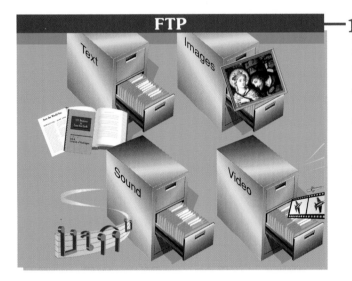

FTP — 12

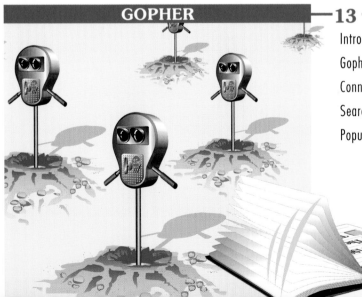

GOPHER — 13

MULTI-PLAYER GAMES

14

INTRANETS

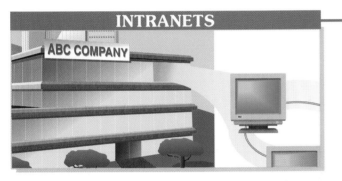

15

GLOSSARY

PGP
Pretty Good Privacy (PGP) is a security program you can use to ensure that no one else can read e-mail messages you send and receive.

Worlds Chat
Worlds Chat is a 3-D chat program that allows you to walk around and talk to other people in a three-dimensional world.

http://www.maran.com

URL
Each Web page has a unique address, called the Uniform Resource Locator (URL). You can instantly display any Web page if you know its URL.

16

The Internet

What is the Internet? In this chapter you will learn what the Internet is, what it has to offer and how information transfers to your computer from around the world.

INTRODUCTION TO THE INTERNET

The Internet is the largest computer system in the world.

The Internet is often called the Net, the Information Superhighway or Cyberspace.

The Internet consists of thousands of connected networks around the world. A network is a collection of computers that are connected to share information.

Each government, company and organization on the Internet is responsible for maintaining its own network.

No one
organization owns
or controls the Internet.
There is no government
regulation and no one
censors the information
on the Internet.

More than 57 million
people in over 150
countries throughout the
world use the Internet today.
If the Internet continues to grow
at the current rate, it is estimated
that everyone in the world will
have access to the Internet
within 10 years.

There is a lot of interesting
and varied information available
on the Internet. Most information
is available free of charge.
Information on the Internet can
travel around the world in less
than one second.

WHAT THE INTERNET OFFERS

ELECTRONIC MAIL

Exchanging electronic mail (e-mail) is the most popular feature on the Internet. You can exchange electronic mail with people around the world, including friends, colleagues, family members, customers and even people you meet on the Internet. Electronic mail is fast, easy, inexpensive and saves paper.

INFORMATION

The Internet gives you access to information on any subject imaginable. You can review newspapers, magazines, academic papers, government documents, television show transcripts, famous speeches, recipes, job listings, works by Shakespeare, airline schedules and much more.

PROGRAMS

Thousands of programs are available on the Internet. These programs include word processors, spreadsheets, games and much more.

ENTERTAINMENT

Hundreds of simple games are available for free on the Internet, including backgammon, chess, poker, football and much more.

The Internet also lets you review current movies, listen to television theme songs, read movie scripts and have interactive conversations with people around the world—even celebrities.

DISCUSSION GROUPS

You can join discussion groups on the Internet to meet people around the world with similar interests. You can ask questions, discuss problems and read interesting stories.

There are thousands of discussion groups on topics such as the environment, food, humor, music, pets, photography, politics, religion, sports and television.

ONLINE SHOPPING

You can order goods and services on the Internet without ever leaving your desk. You can buy items such as books, computer programs, flowers, music CDs, pizza, stocks, used cars and much more.

WHO USES THE INTERNET

People of all ages and backgrounds use the Internet.

Children

The Internet can help children improve their reading and communication skills. Children can send e-mail messages to their friends and explore information on the World Wide Web. Many security products are available that allow children to access the Internet without being exposed to offensive material.

People at Home

There are many services and resources available for people who use the Internet at home. Many people use the Internet at home to access information about their local community. People can often find their local newspapers and information such as movie theater schedules on the Internet.

Students

Many students can access the Internet directly from school. The Internet contains a vast amount of information that can assist students with school projects. Some students can even use the Internet to communicate with their teachers from home.

Researchers

One of the original uses for the Internet was to help researchers and scientists at universities around the world exchange information on joint projects. Information displayed on the World Wide Web allows researchers from different parts of the world to work together.

People at Work

Many people are using the resources available on the Internet to learn how to improve their careers or start a new business. People can also use the Internet to learn new business skills, such as sales or marketing.

There are no long-distance charges when you send or receive information on the Internet.

The Internet is made up of thousands of networks that belong to businesses, government agencies, colleges and universities around the world. These organizations pay to set up and maintain their own parts of the Internet.

Most people pay companies that allow them to connect their computers to the Internet. Once you pay for your connection to the Internet, you can exchange information for free.

When you send information across the Internet, these organizations allow the information to pass through their networks free of charge. This lets you avoid long-distance charges.

WHO OFFERS FREE INFORMATION

Governments

Governments offer information such as federal budgets and NASA reports to educate the public.

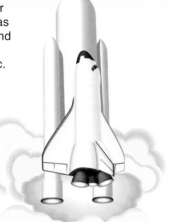

Colleges and Universities

Colleges and universities make information such as journals and software available to the public.

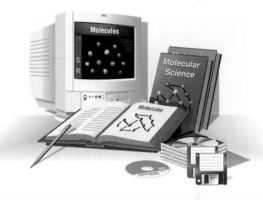

Companies

Companies offer free information to promote a good reputation and to interest you in their products. For example, Ford offers information about its cars and trucks on the Internet.

Individuals

Individuals around the world offer information to give something back to the community. For example, one individual offers dozens of television theme songs that you can access and listen to for free on the Internet.

The Internet was created by combining the ideas and talents of many people. Organizations and individuals have worked together for many years to make the Internet the valuable resource it is today.

ARPANET

In the late 1960s, the U.S. Defense Department created a network that linked military computers together. The network, called ARPANET, was connected in a way that ensured that if one section of the network was damaged, the remaining computers on the network would still be able to communicate with each other.

NSFNET

The National Science Foundation created NSFNET in the mid-1980s. NSFNET used the technology developed for ARPANET to allow universities and schools to connect to each other. By 1987, NSFNET could no longer handle the amount of information that was being transferred. The National Science Foundation improved the network to allow more information to transfer. This improved, high-speed network became the Internet.

Public Access

In the 1980s, most of the people accessing the Internet were scientists and researchers. In the early 1990s, many companies started to offer access to home users. This allowed anyone with a modem and a computer to access the Internet.

The World Wide Web

The World Wide Web was created in the early 1990s by the European Laboratory for Particle Physics. The goal of the World Wide Web was to allow researchers to work together on projects and to make project information easily accessible. The first publicly accessible Web site was created in 1993.

Commercial Sites

By the mid-1990s, over 30 million people had access to the Internet. To reach this huge market, most big companies created their own sites on the World Wide Web to sell or provide information about their products. There are now thousands of companies on the Web.

All computers on the Internet work together to transfer information back and forth around the world.

Packets

When you send information through the Internet, the information is broken down into smaller pieces, called packets. Each packet travels independently through the Internet and may take a different path to arrive at the intended destination.

When information arrives at its destination, the packets are reassembled.

TCP/IP

Transmission Control Protocol/Internet Protocol (TCP/IP) is a language computers on the Internet use to communicate with each other. TCP/IP divides information you send into packets and sends the packets across the Internet. When information arrives at the intended destination, TCP/IP ensures that all the packets arrived safely.

Router

A router is a specialized device that regulates traffic on the Internet and picks the most efficient route for each packet. A packet may pass through many routers before reaching its intended destination.

Backbone

The backbone of the Internet is a set of high-speed data lines that connect major networks all over the world.

Download and Upload Information

When you receive information from another computer on the Internet, you are downloading the information.

When you send information to another computer on the Internet, you are uploading the information.

The Internet is growing and changing at an extraordinary rate. In the future, there will be new ways to access the Internet and different types of information available.

High-Speed Access

Most people who access the Internet from home use a modem. Modems are a very slow way to transfer information. Eventually, most people will have much faster access to the Internet. High-speed access will allow users to watch movies or listen to CD-quality sound on the Internet.

Internet Through the Television

Companies are currently developing a computer that will allow people to use their televisions to access information on the Internet. The computer will be very small and inexpensive. People will be able to use this computer to access the Internet without having to buy expensive computers and monitors.

Users

There are approximately 57 million people on the Internet. By the year 2000, there could be over 400 million people on the Internet. This will make the Internet an even more valuable source for diverse and interesting information.

Virtual Reality

Virtual reality is a computer-generated, three-dimensional world. Virtual reality software allows you to enter a virtual reality world and interact with images. In the future, many resources on the Internet will use virtual reality. You will be able to walk through shopping malls or even visit other planets without ever leaving your home.

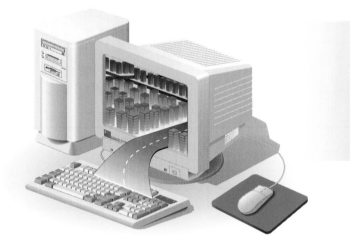

Video E-Mail

Instead of typing e-mail messages to your friends and colleagues, you will eventually be able to record a video and send it to them over the Internet. When your friends and colleagues check their e-mail, they will be able to view the video you sent.

Connect to the Internet

What is required to connect to the Internet? This chapter teaches you about modems, modem alternatives, Internet service providers, commercial online services and much more.

CONNECT TO THE INTERNET

Connecting a computer to the Internet may seem complicated, but it is often a very simple procedure that can be completed in less than 30 minutes.

Computer

You can connect to the Internet using any type of computer, such as an IBM-compatible or a Macintosh. The computer must have specific equipment, such as a modem, to connect to the Internet. Some computers come with the necessary equipment built-in.

Software

You need special software to use the Internet. This software allows your computer to communicate with a company that will provide you with access to the Internet. Most companies that connect you to the Internet offer the software free of charge.

Technical Support

Setting up a connection to the Internet can sometimes be confusing. Make sure the company you use to connect to the Internet has a technical support department.

Find out if you can contact the technical support department in the evenings and on weekends as well as during business hours.

Local or National Access

You can use a local company or a large, national company to connect to the Internet. Local companies may offer special services such as in-home training and access to local organizations. National companies may charge you more but are usually more reliable than local companies.

Shell Access

Shell access lets you connect your computer to the computer of a company that provides access to the Internet. You need a special program, such as Procomm or HyperTerminal, to use shell access.

A modem is a device that lets computers communicate through telephone lines. Modems provide an easy way to access information on the Internet.

Types of Modems

An internal modem is a special circuit board inside a computer. An external modem is a small box that uses a cable to connect to the back of a computer. Internal modems are less expensive than external modems but are more difficult to set up.

Phone Line

A modem plugs into a phone line. You can use the same phone line for telephone and modem calls. When you use a modem to access the Internet, you will not be able to use the phone line for telephone calls. If you are going to spend a lot of time using the Internet, install a second phone line just for the modem.

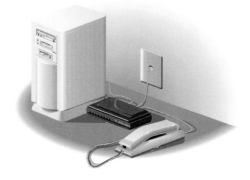

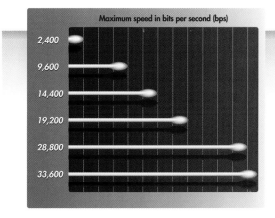

Maximum speed in bits per second (bps)

| 2,400 |
| 9,600 |
| 14,400 |
| 19,200 |
| 28,800 |
| 33,600 |

Speed

Modems transfer information at different speeds. Faster modems transfer files and display Web pages more quickly, so buy the fastest modem you can afford. A modem with a speed of at least 28,800 bps (28.8 Kb/s) is recommended.

Compression

A modem can compress, or squeeze, information being sent to another modem. This speeds up the transfer of information. When information reaches its intended destination, the receiving modem decompresses the information. To use compression, both the sending and receiving modems must use the same type of compression.

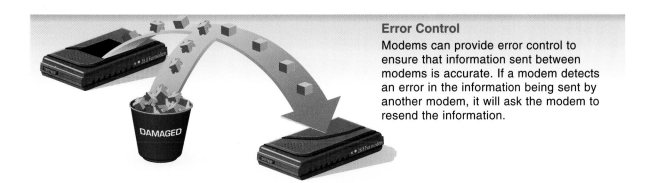

Error Control

Modems can provide error control to ensure that information sent between modems is accurate. If a modem detects an error in the information being sent by another modem, it will ask the modem to resend the information.

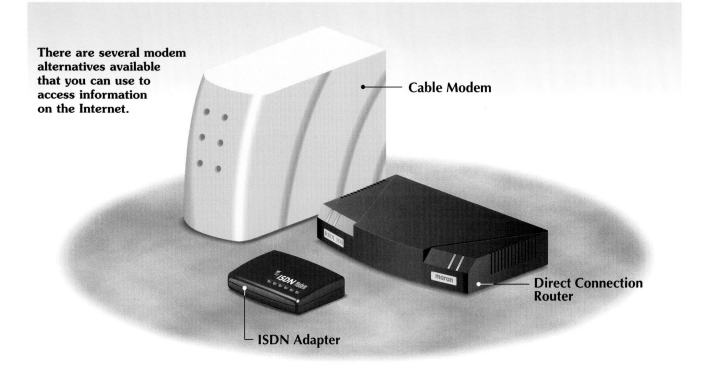

There are several modem alternatives available that you can use to access information on the Internet.

Cable Modem

Direct Connection Router

ISDN Adapter

High-Speed Access

Modem alternatives provide a high-speed connection to the Internet. This allows information to transfer from the Internet to your computer much faster than a regular modem.

Equipment

Alternatives to modems often require special devices or additional computers to connect to the Internet. Many people who use their home computers to connect to the Internet require high-speed connections, so companies are now working to make modem alternatives as easy to set up and use as regular modems.

ISDN

Integrated Services Digital Network (ISDN) is a high-speed digital phone line offered by telephone companies in most urban areas.

ISDN transfers information between the Internet Service Provider (ISP) and your home up to four times faster than a modem.

Cable Modems

A cable modem lets you connect to the Internet with the same cable that attaches to a television set. Cable modems will be offered by many cable companies in the future.

Cable modems transfer information between the cable company and your home more than 200 times faster than a regular modem.

ADSL

Asymmetric Digital Subscriber Line (ADSL) is a high-speed digital phone line that will be offered by local telephone companies in the future.

ADSL can send information to your home more than 200 times faster than a modem. ADSL returns information back to the Internet Service Provider (ISP) at a much slower speed.

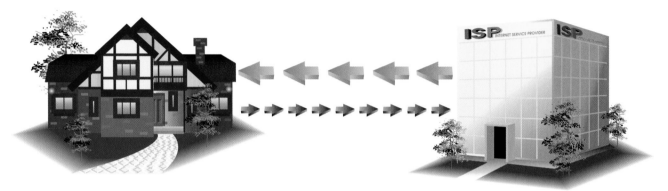

56 Kb/s Modems

A 56 Kb/s modem is a newer type of modem that uses standard telephone lines to connect your computer to the Internet.

A 56 Kb/s modem can send information to your home almost twice as fast as a regular modem. Information transfers back to the Internet Service Provider (ISP) at a slightly slower speed.

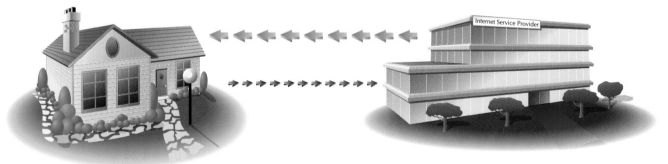

Direct Connection

A direct connection allows you to connect your computer directly to the Internet and provides access to the Internet 24 hours a day. T1 and T3 are the two most popular speeds of direct connection lines.

T1 lines transfer information between the Internet Service Provider (ISP) and your home more than 50 times faster than a modem. T3 lines transfer information approximately 1,500 times faster than a modem.

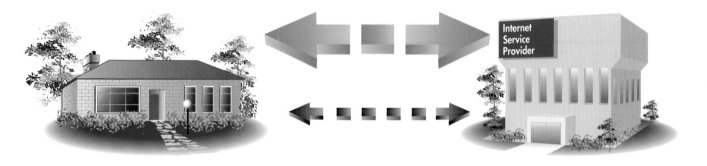

Direct-Broadcast Satellite

The satellite companies that transmit information such as HBO and ShowTime to your television set also offer access to the Internet.

Satellites send information to your home about 14 times faster than a modem.

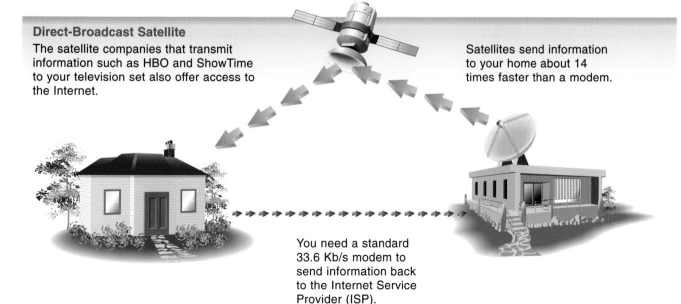

You need a standard 33.6 Kb/s modem to send information back to the Internet Service Provider (ISP).

INTERNET SERVICE PROVIDERS

An Internet Service Provider (ISP) is a company that gives you access to the Internet for a fee.

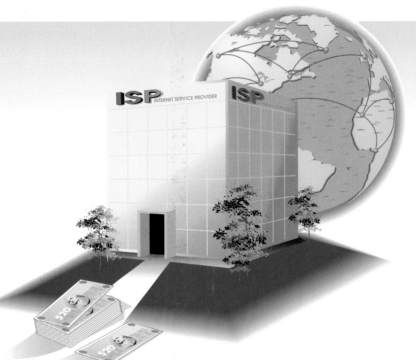

Cost

Using an Internet service provider can be one of the least expensive methods of connecting to the Internet. Many service providers charge only pennies for each hour you use the service. Some ISPs allow you to pay a flat fee for unlimited access to the Internet. Some service providers also charge a fee for setting up your connection to the Internet.

Trial Period

Some Internet service providers allow potential customers to use their service free of charge for a limited time. This allows you to fully evaluate the ISP before paying for the service.

Software

Most Internet service providers offer software that lets you access information on the Internet. This software usually includes a program that lets you exchange e-mail and a program that lets you browse through information.

Full Internet Access

Most Internet service providers allow you to access all the features of the Internet. Other methods of connecting to the Internet may allow you to access only specific Internet features, such as e-mail.

Restrictions

An Internet service provider has control over some of the information available on the Internet. Some service providers block access to information they feel might be offensive or illegal. You should find out if the service provider has any restrictions on information available to you.

Access Numbers

Most Internet service providers let you connect to the Internet by dialing a local telephone number. Some service providers also have a toll free number you can use. This allows you to connect to the Internet without long-distance charges, even when you are traveling.

Modem Speed

When you connect to an Internet service provider, your modem connects to a modem at the ISP. A fast modem can communicate with a slower modem, but they will communicate at the slower speed. Make sure your ISP uses modems that are at least the same speed as your modem.

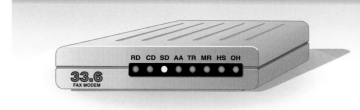

Speed

Most Internet service providers use high-speed lines to connect to the Internet. If many people connect to the ISP at once, information from the Internet will transfer slower to each person. To avoid slow transfers, make sure your ISP uses at least a T1 line to connect to the Internet.

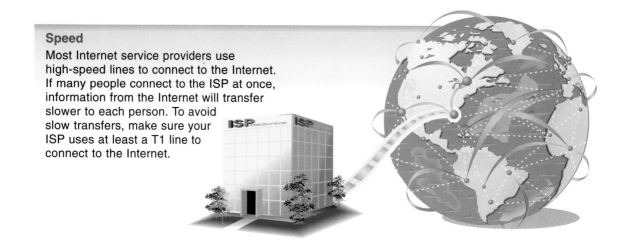

Current Information

Many Internet service providers are now including access to current information from news organizations such as Associated Press and Reuters. Many ISPs provide this feature free of charge.

References

If you intend to spend a lot of time using the Internet, ask the service provider for references from other customers. A good ISP will be able to supply you with a list of customers you may contact. This will help you find out about the reliability and performance of the ISP.

Busy Signals

Ask the Internet service provider how many members there are for each telephone line. More than 10 members for each phone line means you may get a busy signal when you try to connect. If you have the phone number that people use to access the ISP, try dialing it to see if you get a busy signal.

A commercial online service is a company that offers access to the Internet as well as a vast amount of information.

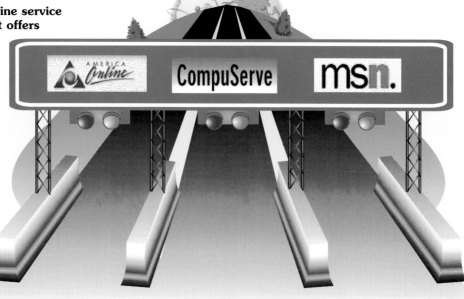

Easy to Set Up

A commercial online service provides software that allows people to connect to the service. This software is usually very easy to install on a computer. Using a commercial online service is often the least complicated way of getting connected to the Internet.

Information

Commercial online services provide access to the Internet as well as a lot of useful and interesting information that is not available anywhere else. Because online services were available before people had easy access to the Internet, the services also provide many well-organized and easy-to-use Internet features, such as e-mail.

AMERICA ONLINE®

**America Online (AOL)®
is one of the most popular
commercial online services.
You can try America Online®
free of charge for a limited
time.**

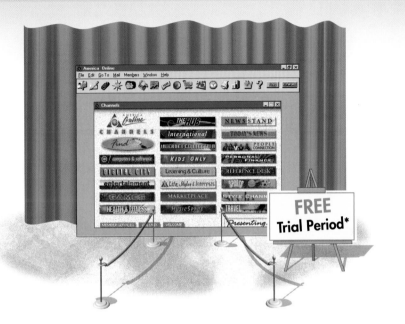

Software

America Online® provides software that
makes it simple for you to connect to
the service. You can also update the
software while you are connected to the
service. This allows you to upgrade to
the latest software versions very easily.

Features

You can use America Online® to search through
an encyclopedia, reserve airline tickets, play
games, manage your investments and more.
AOL® offers discussion groups on many different
topics. The service also regularly invites high-
profile people and celebrities to answer your
questions and respond to your comments.

COMMERCIAL ONLINE SERVICES

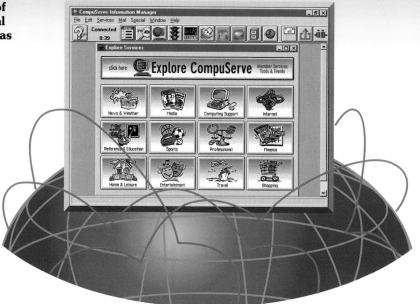

COMPUSERVE

CompuServe is one of the oldest commercial online services and has over 5 million users.

Worldwide Access

CompuServe is available in most countries throughout the world. This makes CompuServe ideal for people who travel frequently but still need access to services such as e-mail. Many businesses use CompuServe to communicate between offices located in different parts of the world.

Access for Children

CompuServe offers easy-to-use software that lets children access CompuServe and the Internet. Children can have fun exploring the Internet and meeting new friends. Parents can set restrictions on their CompuServe accounts so their children will not be able to access offensive material on the Internet.

THE MICROSOFT NETWORK

The Microsoft Network (MSN) is a newer commercial online service. MSN is currently available only to people who use the Windows 95 operating system.

Easy to Set Up

If you use the Windows 95 operating system, you will see an icon on your desktop that allows you to set up MSN. After you select the icon, you follow a step-by-step procedure to quickly and easily connect to MSN.

Easy to Use

MSN was created by the same company that created the Windows 95 operating system. This means that the look and feel of the online service is very similar to the look and feel of other Windows 95 programs. If you are familiar with other Windows 95 programs, you should have no trouble using MSN.

FREENETS

A freenet is a service provider that allows people to access community-based information and the Internet for free.

Worldwide

You can find freenets in many countries around the world. Most large cities and even some rural areas have access to freenets. The easiest way to find out if your community has a freenet is to contact your local library.

Community Information

Most freenets have an area dedicated to informing freenet members about events and organizations in the community. Each freenet also has a separate area where people in the community can announce garage sales and list items they want to buy or sell.

Text-Based

Most freenets allow users to view information on the Internet only as text. Many freenets will be updating their systems in the future to allow users to view images and hear sounds available on the Internet.

Donations

Without donations of computer equipment and money by local businesses and individuals, freenets would not be able to survive. Many freenets offer extra services to their members in return for a donation.

Busy Signals

Freenets are usually very busy. Because freenets depend on donations, they often cannot afford to install additional telephone lines to allow more people to use the freenet at once. When members dial into a freenet, they frequently get a busy signal and must try to connect later.

CONNECT TO THE INTERNET AT WORK

Many companies have
their computer systems
connected to the Internet.
You may be able to use
your computer at work
to access the Internet.

Restrictions

Most companies connected to the Internet do not
offer access to all the features available on the
Internet. Companies may allow employees to use
the Internet only to exchange e-mail or they may
restrict what type of information employees are
allowed to view. Check with your computer
systems administrator at work to find out which
areas of the Internet you can access.

Connect from Home

Many companies allow employees to access
the company computer system from home. If
the company computer system is connected
to the Internet, employees may also be able
to use the Internet from home.

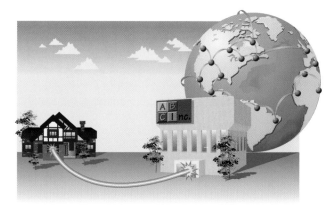

Many people get access to the Internet for the first time while they are at school. Schools have been connected to the Internet since the Internet first began.

Types of Information

Most schools that have been connected to the Internet for a long time use older programs that can display only text. Many schools that are now being connected to the Internet use programs that can also display images and play sounds available on the Internet.

Restrictions

Many colleges and universities have strict limits on Internet access. Students often can access the Internet for only a specific number of hours each week. Access time is usually limited to certain times of the day. There may also be restrictions on the amount of information a student can get from the Internet at one time.

INTERNET CONNECTION TERMS

There are several terms
you need to understand
before connecting your
computer to the Internet.

Servers

A server is a computer that stores information
many people can access. Most of the information
available on the Internet is stored on servers. A
server usually has a name that indicates what
type of information it stores. For example, the
name of a server that stores e-mail messages
usually starts with **mail**.

IP Addresses

Every computer connected to the Internet has a
unique number, called an Internet Protocol (IP)
address. The IP address is made up of four
different numbers separated by periods, such
as 254.234.123.65

Since numbers are hard to remember, most
computers also have a name, such as
"www.company.com", that is easy to understand.
When connecting to a computer, you can type
the IP address or the name of the computer.

TCP/IP

To exchange files and information on the Internet, each computer on the Internet must be able to speak the same language. Transmission Control Protocol/Internet Protocol (TCP/IP) is the language used by computers to transfer information through the Internet.

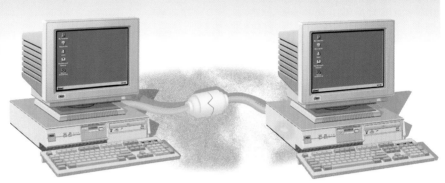

SLIP

Serial Line Internet Protocol (SLIP) allows you to use a modem to connect your home computer to the Internet. When you use SLIP to connect to the Internet, your computer becomes part of the Internet.

PPP

Point-to-Point Protocol (PPP) allows you to use a modem or other device, such as a high-speed cable modem, to connect your home computer to the Internet. PPP also has security features that make it difficult for other people to view the information transferring between two computers.

SERVICE PROVIDER LISTING

There are service providers all over the world that can give you access to the Internet. You can find service providers in telephone books, local newspapers and magazines.

Many providers service Internet users both in Canada and the United States.

America Online®
U.S.A.: 1-800-827-6364
CDN: 1-888-265-4357

CompuServe
1-800-848-8990

Delphi
1-800-695-4005

Microsoft Network
1-800-386-5550

EarthLink Network
1-800-395-8425

Genie
1-800-638-9636

NETCOM
1-800-353-6600

Prodigy
1-800-PRODIGY

UNITED STATES

Atlanta, Georgia
Intergate (770) 429-9599
Epoch Networks (404) 898-2500

Chicago, Illinois
NetWave (312) 335-8038
Tezcat Communications (312) 850-0181

Houston, Texas
Digital Mainstream (713) 364-1819
NetTap (713) 482-3903

Miami, Florida
CyberGate (954) 428-4283
Internet World Information Network (305) 535-3090

Los Angeles, California
LA Internet (213) 932-1999
LightSide (818) 858-9261

New York City, New York
Interport (212) 989-1128
New York Connect.Net (212) 293-2620

Chicago

New York City

Los Angeles

Atlanta

Houston

Miami

INTERNATIONAL

Australia
Geko (02) 9439.1999
Magnadata (02) 9272.9600

Japan
Global Online Japan (03) 5330.9380
Twics Internet (03) 3351.5977

Canada
Internet Direct (416) 233-7150
Pro.NET (604) 688-9282

South Africa
Internet Africa (21) 689.6242
Internet Solutions (11) 447.5566

Ireland
EU Net Ireland (16) 790832
Ireland Online (01) 855.1739

United Kingdom
Atlas Internet (0171) 312.0400
Demon Systems (0181) 349.0063

Information Available on the Internet

What information is available on the Internet? Find out about databases, listings and other resources found on the Internet in this chapter.

Homeowners are usually pleasantly surprised by the positive change in the mood of a room.

In this way, one of the key elements of your home's exterior design can become one of the key elements of its interior design.

terior design

y Brad Hilderley

Concerns about the high costs of interior decorating have led many people to place their dreams on hold.

People experiencing second thoughts will be relieved to know that one of the greatest design tools at their disposal is free: natural lighting.

Dark, gloomy rooms can often be brought to life by the addition of one or more skylights or by enlarging existing windows.

26

You can find information presented in many different ways on the Internet.

Text

There are many files on the Internet that display only text. You can display the information in many of these text files in any program that lets you view or edit text, such as a word processor.

Text files often provide instructions or additional information for software programs and other types of files available on the Internet. These types of text files usually have names such as fileid.diz, readme.1st or info.txt

HTML

HTML stands for HyperText Markup Language and is a language used to display information on the Internet.

You can use a program called a Web browser to view the information displayed in an HTML document. HTML documents on the Internet usually have the .htm or .html extension.

Sound

There are many sound files available on the Internet, such as speeches, music and promotional material for companies. You need a sound card and speakers for your computer before you can listen to sound files from the Internet.

Video

In the past, access to the Internet was so slow that any video clips had to be very short and were usually poor quality. Now that many people have faster access to the Internet, you can get much better quality video on the Internet.

Video clips are also becoming more widely available. Most computers can play video clips from the Internet.

STREAMING DATA

Often when you transfer information from the Internet to your computer, you must wait until all the information has transferred before you can view or play the information.

Streaming data is a system that lets you view or play information while the file is still transferring to your computer. Sound, video and HTML files often use streaming data to transfer to your computer.

DATABASES ON THE INTERNET

A database is a large collection of information. Many companies and organizations on the Internet allow people to access the information stored in their databases.

Types of Information

Databases on the Internet offer many different types of information. You can find databases containing entertaining information, such as jokes and pictures. You can also find databases of very useful information, such as software updates and registered patents.

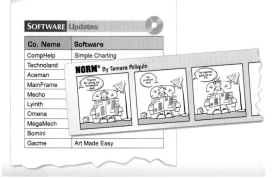

Cost

You must pay a fee to access the information in many databases available on the Internet. Some databases will let you access a small amount of information in a database free of charge. This allows you to try out the database before paying to access the information.

There are many different
lists of information available
on the Internet. You can
use the Internet to easily
find information.

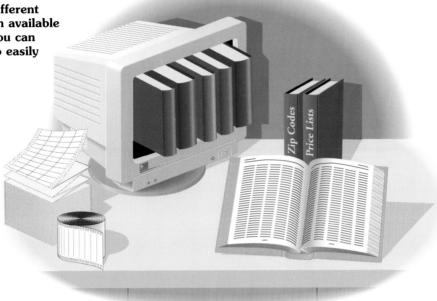

Directories

A directory is a list of information
such as zip codes or electronic mail
addresses. Many phone companies
are now making phone books available
in directories on the Internet.

Catalogs

Most companies that sell or advertise
products make their product catalogs
available on the Internet. A catalog can
be a simple price list or a collection of
text, video and sound similar to a television
advertisement. Catalogs available on the
Internet are easier to update than printed
catalogs so they usually contain more
accurate information.

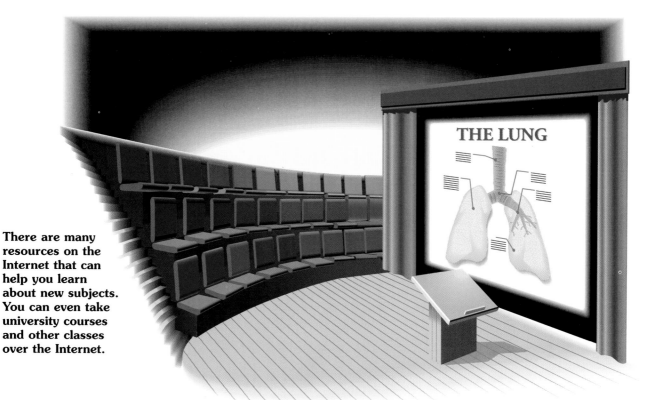

There are many resources on the Internet that can help you learn about new subjects. You can even take university courses and other classes over the Internet.

Product Support

Many companies use the Internet to provide product support for their customers. You can often get product manuals and specifications over the Internet. Many companies provide this type of information free of charge. This means that customers do not have to use older methods, such as the telephone or regular mail, to get product support.

Reference Tools

There are many types of reference tools now available on the Internet. You can find dictionaries for many different languages, encyclopedias, books of famous quotations and much more. Most reference tools on the Internet are available free of charge.

Step-By-Step Instruction

The World Wide Web consists of many documents that can be joined together in a specific order. This makes the Web very useful for instructional guides. Each step can be displayed as a single document. You can move through the steps one at a time, at your own pace. You can also print out each document and use the pages for reference later.

Schools

Many schools and universities offer courses you can complete using the Internet. You can send projects and essays to the instructor by electronic mail. The school or university will often make lecture notes and diagrams for the course available on the Internet.

Live Instruction

It is currently quite easy to transfer sound and video over the Internet. Students will soon be able to use their computers at home to view and participate in classes taking place at a school or university. This will be very useful for students who are ill or who live far away from the school.

Web broadcasting makes it easy to get information that interests you from the Internet. Instead of searching for information, you can use a Web broadcaster to automatically collect the information and deliver it to your computer.

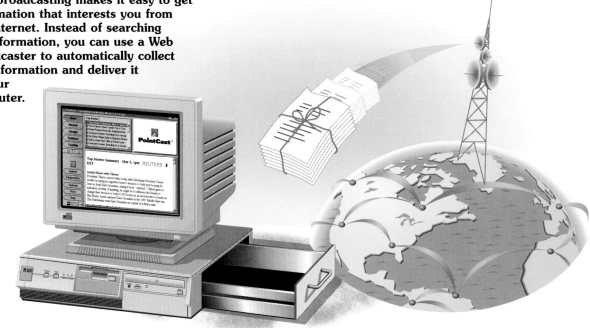

How it Works

Web broadcasting uses the same type of technology to transfer information to your computer as television stations use to transmit programs to your television. Web broadcasting is often referred to as Push technology because information is being "pushed" from the Web broadcaster to your computer.

Agents

An agent is a software program used by a Web broadcaster to collect information and then display the information on your screen. An agent allows you to specify the type of information you want to view and then transfers the information from the Web broadcaster to your computer.

Access

You must be connected to the Internet before you can receive information from a Web broadcaster. The company or organization you work for may have a connection to the Internet, but some companies restrict employees from accessing Web broadcast information services.

Channels

Web broadcasters arrange related information into groups, called channels. A Web broadcaster may group football, baseball and basketball information into a sports channel. You can subscribe to the sports channel to receive all the latest scores, team rosters and player interviews.

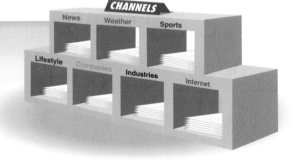

Newsfeeds

A newsfeed is a collection of news information. Each newsfeed focuses on one category of news information such as financial reports, weather conditions or current events.

Most Web broadcasters allow users to access information provided by newsfeeds. Some of the most popular newsfeeds are provided by the Associated Press and Reuters.

THE POINTCAST NETWORK

The PointCast Network is one of the most popular Web broadcasting networks available on the Internet. More than one million people use the PointCast Network.

You can get the PointCast Network on the World Wide Web at:
http://www.pointcast.com

Cost

You can use the PointCast Network free of charge. The PointCast Network sells 30 second animated commercials to generate income to pay for the service. When you click on an advertisement, the advertiser's Web site will appear on your screen.

Updates

The PointCast Network transfers the latest news and information to your computer. You can have the PointCast Network send updated information to your computer automatically or only when you ask for an update. You must be connected to the Internet to receive updates from the PointCast Network.

Stock Market Information

The PointCast Network provides information from stock markets located across North America. You can customize the PointCast Network to display the stock prices of only the companies that interest you. The stock market information supplied by the PointCast Network is approximately 15 minutes old when it reaches your computer.

News

The PointCast Network allows you to access many newspaper and magazine articles. Some articles display pictures and photographs.

Many well-known publications supply articles to the PointCast Network, such as The New York Times, The Boston Globe and Time magazine.

Screen Saver

The PointCast Network has a SmartScreen feature that lets you use the PointCast Network as your screen saver.

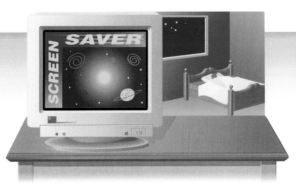

Any time your computer is idle, the PointCast Network will automatically begin displaying the latest headlines and other information you select.

The World Wide Web

What is the World Wide Web? This chapter introduces you to the Web and what it has to offer. You will learn about Web browsers, multimedia on the Web, shopping on the Web and much more.

INTRODUCTION TO THE WEB

The World Wide Web is part of the Internet. The Web consists of a huge collection of documents stored on computers around the world.

The World Wide Web is also called the Web, WWW or W3.

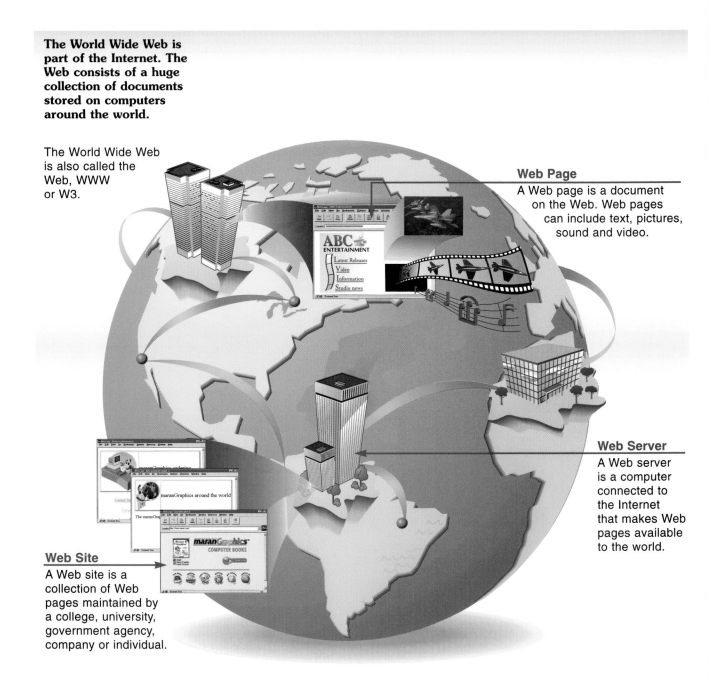

Web Page

A Web page is a document on the Web. Web pages can include text, pictures, sound and video.

Web Server

A Web server is a computer connected to the Internet that makes Web pages available to the world.

Web Site

A Web site is a collection of Web pages maintained by a college, university, government agency, company or individual.

Each Web page has a unique address, called the Uniform Resource Locator (URL). You can instantly display any Web page if you know its URL.

■ All Web page URLs start with http (HyperText Transfer Protocol).

Web pages are hypertext documents. A hypertext document contains highlighted text that connects to other pages on the Web. You can select highlighted text on a Web page to display a page located on the same computer or a computer across the city, country or world.

Highlighted text allows you to easily navigate through a vast amount of information by jumping from one Web page to another.

WEB BROWSERS

A Web browser is a program that lets you view and explore information on the World Wide Web.

HTML Support

HyperText Markup Language (HTML) is a computer language used to create Web pages. There are several versions of HTML. Each new version allows more features, such as multimedia, on Web pages. If your Web browser does not support the latest version, you will not be able to use the newest features. Version 3.2 is the latest version of HTML.

Beta Versions

A beta version of a Web browser is an early version of the program that is not quite ready for sale. Many companies let people use and test the beta versions of their Web browsers before releasing the official versions. Beta versions of Web browsers sometimes contain errors.

Bookmarks

Most Web browsers have a feature
called bookmarks or favorites. This
feature lets you store the addresses
of Web pages you frequently visit.
Bookmarks save you from having
to remember and constantly retype
your favorite Web page addresses.

History List

When you are browsing through pages
on the World Wide Web, it can be
difficult to keep track of the locations
of pages you have visited. Most Web
browsers include a history list that
allows you to quickly return to any
Web page you have recently visited.

Speed

Web browsers display Web pages at
different speeds. Many factors, such
as the type of computer and modem
you use, determine how fast a Web
browser will display pages. Before
buying a Web browser, try out a few
browsers on your computer to see
which browser displays Web pages
the fastest.

NETSCAPE NAVIGATOR

Netscape Navigator is currently the most popular Web browser used to view Web pages.

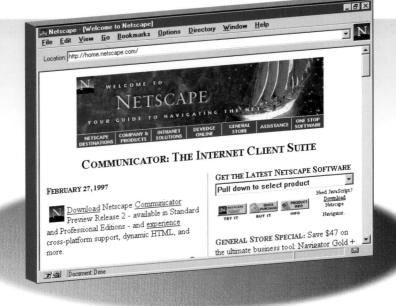

Versatile

Navigator is available for computers running many different operating systems, including OS/2, Macintosh, Windows and Unix. Navigator is also available in over 10 different languages.

You can get Netscape Navigator at the following Web site:

http://home.netscape.com

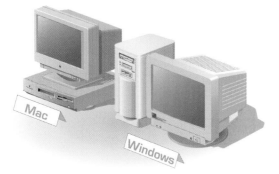

Plug-Ins

A plug-in is a program that performs a task that a Web browser cannot perform on its own. You can find plug-ins that let you view high-quality video, spell check your e-mail messages and display three-dimensional Web pages. Software companies can easily add plug-ins to Navigator to enhance the Web browser.

Netscape Extensions

HyperText Markup Language (HTML) is the name of the programming language used to create Web pages. Netscape continually makes improvements, called Netscape extensions, to HTML.

These improvements allow Web pages to include such features as video and sound. Navigator is currently the only Web browser that can properly display Web pages containing Netscape extensions.

E-Mail and News

Navigator is currently the only Web browser with an e-mail program and a newsreader built-in. These built-in features are easy to learn and use because they have the same look and feel as the Web browser.

Create Web Pages

Navigator Gold is a version of Netscape Navigator that allows you to easily create pages for the World Wide Web.

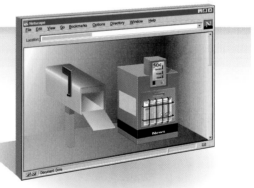

You can also use Navigator Gold to easily transfer your Web pages to a Web server.

MICROSOFT INTERNET EXPLORER

Microsoft Internet Explorer is a newer Web browser that is quickly becoming one of the most popular.

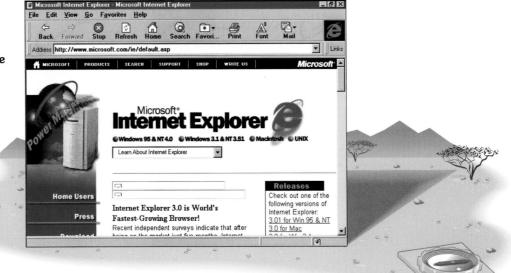

Easy to Use

Internet Explorer was created by the same company that created the Windows operating systems. This means that the look and feel of Internet Explorer is very similar to the look and feel of other Windows programs. If you are familiar with other Windows programs, you should find the Web browser easy to learn and use.

Cost

You can get Internet Explorer free of charge when you buy the Microsoft Windows operating system. Internet Explorer is also available for computers that use the Macintosh operating system.

You can get Internet Explorer free of charge at the following Web site:

http://www.microsoft.com/ie

Customize the Display

Internet Explorer allows you to customize the display of the Web browser.

You can change the size and position of the toolbar on the screen. You can even add your favorite Web pages to the toolbar.

Restrict Access

Internet Explorer allows you to use a rating system to restrict access to Web sites containing offensive material. This allows parents to control the information their children view on the World Wide Web.

E-Mail and News

Internet Explorer has an available e-mail program and newsreader. You can easily exchange information between the Web browser, the e-mail program and the newsreader.

This allows you to send e-mail messages containing articles from newsgroups or information from Web pages.

LYNX

Lynx is one of the oldest Web browsers available. Lynx is usually found on text-based computers, such as computers using Unix and MS-DOS.

```
                                      Future Books from maranGraphics
(p1 of 2)

    [LINK]

Future Books from maranGraphics


    Here is a list of some of the books we will be releasing
    shortly. If you have any questions or comments about these
    books, please send an e-mail message to www@maran.com

Title                        Date              Pages    Comments
Office 97 Simplified         Now Available!    368      Full color
Teach Yourself Office 97     Now Available!    368      Full color
Word 97 Simplified           March 1997        240      Full color
Excel 97 Simplified          April 1997        240      Full color


-- press space for next page --
    Arrow keys: Up and Down to move. Right to follow a link; Left
back.
    H)elp O)ptions P)rint G)o M)ain screen Q)uit /=search [delete
list
```

Restrictions

Lynx is a text-based Web browser. This means that Lynx users do not have access to many of the features available on the World Wide Web. If you use Lynx, you will not be able to use the Web browser to view images, hear sound or watch animation displayed on Web pages.

Advantages

Because Lynx displays only text, Web pages transfer to your computer and appear on your screen very quickly. This can save you time and money. Web pages that display only text can also be less distracting than pages that display multimedia.

Cost

Lynx can run on very inexpensive computers or computers with old, outdated equipment. Because Lynx does not require powerful computers to run, almost everyone can have access to the World Wide Web.

You can get Lynx free of charge at the following Web site:

http://www.lynx.browser.org

E-Mail and News

You can specify which e-mail program and newsreader you want to use with Lynx. When you select an e-mail or newsgroup link on a Web page, Lynx will automatically start the e-mail program or newsreader.

Accessibility Options

Lynx has several features that make the Web browser easy to use for people with physical disabilities. You can make text easier to view on the screen by displaying the text at a larger size.

You can also number the links on a Web page. This lets you select a link by pressing a number key on your keyboard.

Frames

Some Web pages divide information into rectangular sections, called frames. Each frame displays a different Web page.

Forms

Some Web pages include forms that let you enter information. The information you type into a form travels across the Internet to the computer that maintains the page. Many companies use forms to allow readers to express their opinions, ask questions or order goods and services.

Tables

Some Web pages display information in tables. A table organizes information into an easy-to-follow, attractive format. Tables in Web pages often display lists of information, such as financial data, telephone listings and price lists. Tables can include images as well as text.

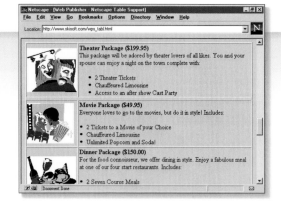

You can buy products and services on the Web without ever leaving your desk.

There are thousands of products you can buy on the Web, such as clothing, flowers, office supplies and computer programs.

The Web also offers a range of services, such as banking and financial or real estate advice.

Companies

Thousands of companies have Web sites where you can get product information and buy products and services online.

You can view a list of companies on the Web at the following site:

http://www.cio.com/central/businesses.html

Shopping Malls

There are shopping malls on the Web where you can view and buy products and services offered by many different companies.

You can view a list of shopping malls on the Web at the following site:

http://nsns.com/MouseTracks/HallofMalls.html

SECURITY ON THE WEB

Many Web pages require you to enter confidential information about yourself to use the services they offer or buy their products. There are secure pages on the Web that will protect confidential information sent over the Internet.

When you send information over the Internet, the information may pass through many computers before reaching its destination.

If you are not connected to a secure Web page, people may be able to view the information you send.

Secure Web Pages

Secure Web pages work with Web browsers that support security features to create an almost unbreakable security system. When you connect to a secure Web page, other people on the Internet cannot view the information you transfer.

Visit Secure Web Pages

When a reader visits a secure Web page, the Web browser will usually display a solid key or a lock at the bottom corner of the screen. This indicates that the Web page is secure.

Internet Explorer   Netscape Navigator

Credit Cards

Many people feel it is unsafe to transmit credit card numbers over the Internet. In fact, sending a credit card number over a secure connection can be safer than giving the number to an unknown person over the phone or by fax.

Companies

Some people work at home and use the Internet to connect to computers at the office. Secure Web pages allow employees to access confidential information that companies would not make available over connections that are not secure.

Banking

Many banks allow you to access your banking information over the Web. You can pay bills, transfer money between accounts and even apply for a loan.

Banking information is one of the most confidential types of information. Banks use secure Web pages to keep this information secret.

A Web page can contain text, images, sound, video and animation.

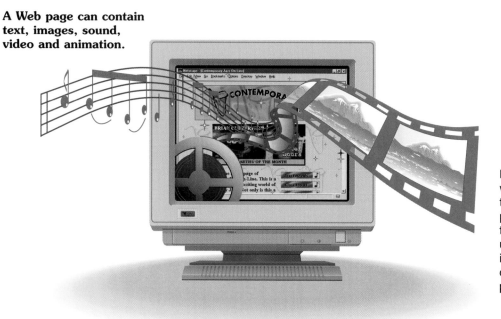

Multimedia is an effective way of attracting attention to information on a Web page. Many companies that advertise on the Web use a combination of text, images, sound and video or animation to sell their products and services.

Transfer Time

Some files take a while to transfer to your computer. A Web page usually shows you the size of a file to give you an indication of how long the file will take to transfer.

Use this chart as a guide to determine how long a file will take to transfer to your computer.

	File Size		Time
Bytes	Kilobytes (KB)	Megabytes (MB)	(estimated)
10,000,000	10,000	10	1 hour
5,000,000	5,000	5	30 minutes
2,500,000	2,500	2.5	15 minutes

This chart is based on transferring files with a 28,800 bps modem. A modem with a speed of 14,400 bps or lower will transfer files more slowly than shown in the chart.

Text

You can view documents on the Web such as newspapers, magazines, plays, famous speeches and television show transcripts.

Text transfers quickly to your computer, so you do not have to wait long to read text on a Web page.

Images

You can view images on the Web such as album covers, pictures of celebrities and famous paintings.

Sound

You can hear sound on the Web such as TV theme songs, movie soundtracks, sound effects and historical speeches.

You need a sound card and speakers to hear sound on the Web.

Video and Animation

You can view video and animation on the Web such as movie clips, cartoons and interviews with celebrities.

Video and animation files often take a while to transfer to your computer.

RealAudio is a program that lets you listen to sound such as live radio shows, music or interviews on the World Wide Web.

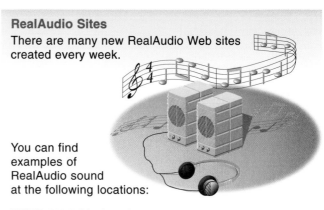

You can get
the RealAudio sound
player at the following Web site:

http://www.realaudio.com

Streaming Audio

RealAudio uses a system called streaming audio to transfer sound to your computer. Other programs that play sound must transfer the entire sound file to your computer before you can listen to the sound. With streaming audio, you can listen to the sound while the file is transferring.

RealAudio Sites

There are many new RealAudio Web sites created every week.

You can find
examples of
RealAudio sound
at the following locations:

WGRR 103.5 Cincinnati

http://www.wgrr1035.com/cgi-bin/rightnow/rightnow

National Museum of American Art

http://www.nmaa.si.edu/masterdir/pagesub/whatnew.html

Microsoft Music Central

http://MusicCentral.msn.com/Default.asp

Shockwave is a program that allows you to view animated images using your Web browser. Many pages on the Web display Shockwave animation.

You can get the Shockwave program at the following Web site:

http://www.macromedia.com

Animation

Many companies use Shockwave to display animated advertisements for their products on the World Wide Web. Some Shockwave animations now also include sound. Advertisements containing both sound and animation have much more impact on the Web.

Games

Shockwave is often used to create interactive games for the Web.

You can find some good examples of interactive, animated games at the following Web sites:

Coca-Cola

http://www.cocacola.com/digitalworkout

Sunny Delight

http://www.sunnyd.com

Shockwave Stuff

http://www.gw2k.com/cool/kids/paintbox/shocpage.htm

Java is a programming language that allows you to create animated and interactive Web pages.

A Java program used in a Web page is called a Java applet. You can write a Java applet yourself or use one of the existing applets available on the Web.

How Java Works

Java applets are stored on a Web server. When a reader displays a Web page containing a Java applet, the applet transfers from the Web server to the reader's computer and then runs. Some Java applets take a long time to transfer.

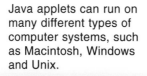

Java applets can run on many different types of computer systems, such as Macintosh, Windows and Unix.

Web Browsers

Before viewing a Java applet on a Web page, a reader must have a Web browser that can run Java applets. Most new Web browsers can run Java applets.

Web Page Enhancements

Most people use Java applets to enhance their Web pages. Many applets are used to display moving text or simple animation.

You can view a collection of Java applets at the following Web site:

http://www.gamelan.com

Interactive Web Pages

People often include Java applets in their Web pages to allow readers to interact with each other on the Web. Some Java applets allow readers to play games or chat with other people.

Programs

You can use Java to write complex programs such as word processing, spreadsheet and drawing programs. These types of Java applets are very large. Most people do not include this type of Java applet in their Web pages because the applets take too long to transfer.

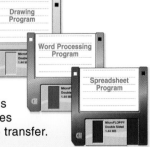

JAVASCRIPT

JavaScript is a programming language that is mainly used for Web page enhancements, such as displaying scrolling messages and fading-in Web pages.

Although the names are similar, JavaScript and Java have very little in common. JavaScript is easier to learn than Java.

How JavaScript Works

JavaScript instructions are placed in the HTML document. You can write JavaScript instructions yourself or use existing JavaScript instructions available on the Web. You can view examples of JavaScript at the following Web site:

http://www.gamelan.com

Web Browsers

Before viewing JavaScript on a Web page, a reader must have a Web browser that can run JavaScript instructions. Most new Web browsers can run JavaScript.

ActiveX is a newer
technology developed
by Microsoft to help
you improve your
Web pages.

Reasons for Using ActiveX

ActiveX is commonly used in Web pages to
add pop-up menus that instantly display a list
of options.

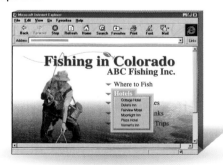

You can also use ActiveX to include animated
images and information from popular programs,
such as Microsoft Word or Microsoft Excel, in
your Web pages.

Web Browsers

Before viewing a Web page that includes ActiveX
features, a reader must have a Web browser that
supports ActiveX.
Microsoft Internet
Explorer has
built-in support
for ActiveX.

Some Web browsers, including Netscape Navigator,
currently do not have built-in support. Readers who
want to use ActiveX with Navigator can get a special
program at the following Web site:

http://www.ncompasslabs.com

Virtual Reality Modeling Language (VRML) allows you to create three-dimensional objects and environments, called VRML worlds.

VRML Viewers

A VRML viewer lets you use a mouse or keyboard to move through three-dimensional areas or walk around objects in a VRML world. To display a VRML world, a Web browser must support VRML. Most new browsers support VRML.

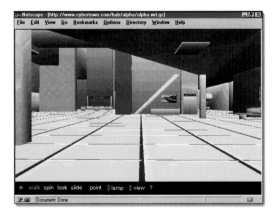

VRML Editors

Creating VRML worlds requires a lot of time. A VRML editor is a program that can help you create VRML worlds. One of the most popular VRML editors is Caligari Pioneer, which is available at the following Web site:

http://www.caligari.com

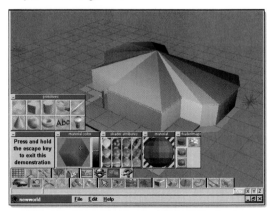

REASONS FOR USING VRML

Entertainment

You can use VRML to create three-dimensional towns, movies and games. When playing a VRML game, you can compete against other people on the Web.

You can find entertaining VRML worlds at the following Web sites:

http://www.cybertown.com/3dvd.html

http://www.virtualvegas.com/vrml/vrml1.html

Product Demonstrations

Companies often use VRML to show their products. You can walk around products and view them from any angle. This gives you control that you do not have when viewing television or magazine advertisements.

Two companies that allow you to view their products using VRML are at the following Web sites:

http://www.netvision.net.il/~teldor/vrml.html

http://www.asia-online.com.sg/perfection/es300/features.html

Training

In the future, there will be VRML worlds that allow people to use the Internet to train at home instead of going to a classroom.

Companies will also create VRML worlds to provide instruction on tasks such as servicing electronic products or repairing cars.

CHILDREN AND THE WEB

Most of the information on the Web is meant to educate or entertain readers, but some sites may contain material you find offensive. Children should be carefully monitored when browsing the World Wide Web.

TYPES OF INAPPROPRIATE INFORMATION

Pictures

There are many sites on the Web that display pictures meant for adult users. Most adult-oriented sites require verification that users are adults, but the sites often display sample pictures on the first page of the Web site.

Text Files

There are many text files on the Web describing everything from causing mischief at school to making explosives. These types of text files often appeal to teenagers and are usually found at Web sites distributing banned or censored books. These Web sites generally do not have any restrictions on who can access the text files.

HOW TO RESTRICT ACCESS

Adult Supervision

Constant adult supervision is the best way to ensure that children do not access inappropriate information on the Web.

Ground Rules

- No foul language
- No X-rated Web sites
- **No alt newsgroups**
- No responding to e-mail from strangers

Before each Web browsing session, the adult and child should decide the purpose of the session, such as researching a school project. This will help set ground rules for browsing and make the time spent on the Web more productive.

Browser Restrictions

Some Web browsers have built-in restrictions. Users can view only sites that have been approved by a rating system similar to the system used to rate films and motion pictures. You can decide what rating level is appropriate for your children.

Restriction Programs

You can buy programs that restrict access to all areas of the World Wide Web and most areas of the Internet. Most of these programs are relatively new, but they are efficient at restricting access to offensive material.

You can find restriction programs at the following Web sites:

Net Nanny
http://www.netnanny.com

Cyber Patrol
http://www.microsys.com

Search the World Wide Web

How can information of interest be found on the World Wide Web? In this chapter you will learn how search tools and search programs can help you find information quickly and easily.

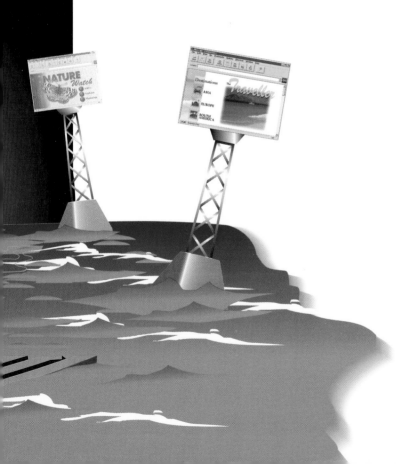

INTRODUCTION TO SEARCHING THE WEB

Search tools help you find information on the World Wide Web quickly and easily.

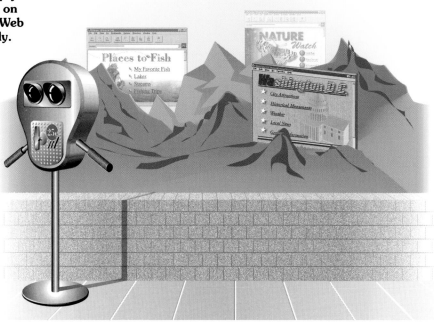

Free

You do not have to pay to use a search tool to find information on the World Wide Web. Many search tools sell advertising space on their Web sites to generate income to pay for the service.

Search Newsgroups

Many search tools let you search for information in discussion groups, or newsgroups. This lets you find even more information about a subject that interests you. Most search tools store information that has been posted to newsgroups for a few weeks.

Databases

Search tools store information collected from Web pages in a database. When searching for information on the Web, you enter a description of the information you want to find. The search tool then searches the database for the information you requested.

Directories

Directories, or meta-indexes, are databases that store information about Web sites that people have reviewed and cataloged.

Directories are often more accurate and organized than other types of search tools.

Search Engines

Search engines use a program, called a robot, to scan the Web for new and updated pages. Since hundreds of new pages are created each day, it is impossible for a robot to catalog every new page on the Web.

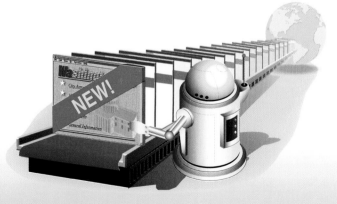

FIND WEB PAGES WITH ALTAVISTA

With over 30 million entries, AltaVista is one of the biggest and most popular search tools on the Web.

AltaVista is located at:
http://www.altavista.digital.com

HOW ALTAVISTA WORKS

AltaVista uses a robot program called Scooter to find new and updated pages on the World Wide Web. When Scooter finds a Web page that did not exist before or has changed, the robot copies all the text from the Web page and stores it in the AltaVista index.

When searching in AltaVista, you type words or phrases to describe the information you want to find. AltaVista searches the index for Web pages containing the words or phrase you typed and displays a list of the pages it found. You can then select the Web pages you want to visit from the list.

TYPES OF ALTAVISTA SEARCHES

Simple Search

The simple search is the most popular type of AltaVista search.

When performing a simple search, you type words separated by a space or a phrase surrounded by quotation marks.

Advanced Search

An advanced search gives you more control over your searches. When you type a word or phrase in the Results Ranking Criteria area, AltaVista will display Web pages containing the word or phrase you specified at the top of the list.

Commands

When performing an advanced search, you can use special commands to make your search even more precise.

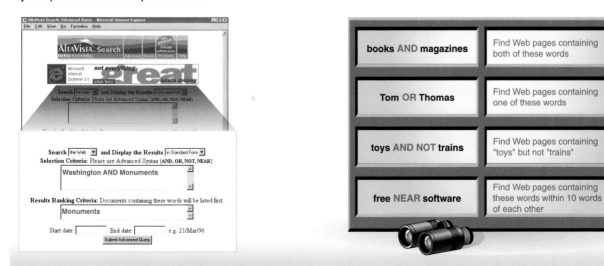

books AND magazines	Find Web pages containing both of these words
Tom OR Thomas	Find Web pages containing one of these words
toys AND NOT trains	Find Web pages containing "toys" but not "trains"
free NEAR software	Find Web pages containing these words within 10 words of each other

FIND WEB PAGES WITH EXCITE

Excite is one of the most comprehensive search tools available on the Web. Excite also offers a reference section and online maps for locations across the U.S. and around the world.

Excite is located at:
http://www.excite.com

HOW EXCITE WORKS

Database

There are currently over 50 million Web pages in the Excite database. When you enter the information you want to find, Excite searches all the Web pages in its database and then displays a list of pages containing the information you requested.

Search Results

When you perform a search, Excite displays 10 results at a time. Excite also displays a rating beside the title of each Web page to indicate how successful the search was. A 100% rating indicates that the Web page definitely contains the word or phrase you entered.

EXCITE SEARCH OPTIONS

Phrases

You can search for a specific group of words in Excite. To find a specific phrase, type quotation marks around the group of words you want to find.

Advanced Search

You can make your search more precise by typing a symbol in front of a word. Make sure you do not leave any spaces between the symbol and the following word.

| cars +wheels | Find Web pages containing "wheels" but not necessarily "cars" |
| +painting -watercolor | Find Web pages containing "painting" but not "watercolor" |

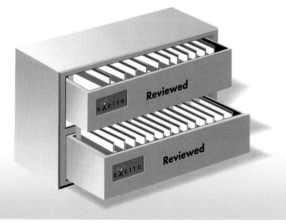

Reviews

You can browse through over 60,000 Web pages that have been reviewed by the Excite staff. Although the review section does not contain as many Web pages as the main database, the reviewed pages are better organized and provide you with more information about the pages.

FIND WEB PAGES WITH LYCOS

Lycos is a search tool that allows you to find a lot of interesting information on the Web. The Lycos database contains over 70 million Web pages.

Lycos is located at:
http://www.lycos.com

HOW LYCOS WORKS

When searching in Lycos, you type a description of the information you are looking for. Lycos searches its database for Web pages containing the words you entered and then displays the results.

Lycos lets you enter special symbols with the words you type to help make your search more precise.

LYCOS FEATURES

Pictures and Sounds

You can use Lycos to easily search for images and sounds. When Lycos enters Web pages into the database, Lycos also indexes any sound, image and animation files it finds.

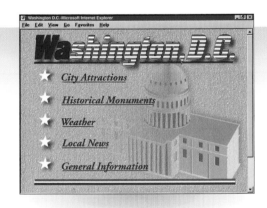

City Guide

Lycos allows you to easily find information about cities throughout the United States. You can quickly access local information, history, statistics and much more about each city in the City Guide. The guide also contains links to Web sites containing more information about each city.

Road Maps

You can use Lycos to find and display road maps for an address within the United States. When you enter a street address or a zip code, Lycos will display a map showing a detailed view of the surrounding area.

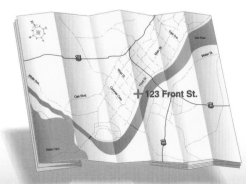

FIND WEB PAGES WITH YAHOO!

Yahoo! was started by two students as a way to keep track of their favorite Web sites. It has quickly grown into one of the best search tools on the Web.

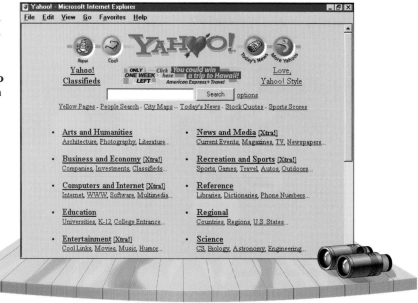

Yahoo! is located at:
http://www.yahoo.com

Categories

Every Web site in the Yahoo! directory is reviewed and cataloged by the people at Yahoo!. Web sites containing similar information are grouped together in categories. You can browse through the categories and subcategories until you find Web pages containing the information you want.

Ratings

When people review Web sites for the Yahoo! catalog, they also check out the quality of information in the Web sites. Yahoo! displays a small picture of a pair of sunglasses beside any site that provides good information. When searching Yahoo!, you should try Web sites displaying sunglasses first.

News Headlines

Yahoo! allows you to read the latest news stories from around the world. Yahoo! gathers the information from various news sources and then displays the information on Web pages. The information is updated approximately once an hour.

Special Categories

Yahoo! provides several special Web page categories you can browse through. You can view a listing of "Cool" sites, the picks of the week or the favorite sites of the day.

Personalized Information

You can select topics that interest you, such as sports and entertainment, and have Yahoo! create a custom Web page for you. Your custom Yahoo! page will automatically display only the information you requested. Information such as weather and news stories are updated on a regular basis.

Search programs are
programs you run on
your own computer.
Search programs are
useful to anyone who
searches the Web for
information frequently.

Efficient

Using search programs is an efficient
way to search for information on the
Web. Many search programs allow you
to perform searches while you complete
other tasks. You can also schedule
your searches for times that are more
convenient, such as during the night.

Comprehensive

Search programs often submit information you
request to several search tools on the Web.
One search tool may offer more information than
another search tool but may update Web pages
less often. By using a search program, you can
search all types of search tools at once.

SEARCH PROGRAMS

Teleport Pro

Teleport Pro can help you perform in-depth Web searches. When you enter a word you want to find, Teleport Pro will search a Web site you specify to find all the Web pages containing the word.

Teleport Pro is available at:

http://www.tenmax.com

WebFerret

WebFerret is one of the fastest search programs available. You can often get results from a search within a few seconds.

WebFerret is available at:

http://www.vironix.com/netferret/webferret.htm

WebSeeker

WebSeeker allows you to enter a word and then submits the word to more than 20 search tools on the Web. WebSeeker then sorts and displays the results of the search. WebSeeker can also monitor Web pages and inform you when the pages are updated.

WebSeeker is available at:

http://www.ffg.com/seeker.html

Create Web Pages

What is required to create Web pages? This chapter introduces you to the process of creating Web pages and making them available to the world. You will also find examples of impressive Web sites.

REASONS FOR PUBLISHING WEB PAGES

Publishing your own pages on the World Wide Web allows millions of people around the world to view your information.

Present Information of Interest

Many people use the Web to display information about a topic or range of related topics that interest them. Many Web pages are devoted to movie stars, sports teams and celebrities. People often include sounds and pictures from their favorite television shows in their Web pages.

Learn a New Skill

In just a few years, the World Wide Web has quickly grown from a small number of Web pages to millions of pages. By learning how to create and publish pages on the Web, you gain a skill that could be valuable in your current or future career.

Technical Support

Companies often let you contact their technical support department through their Web site. If you have a problem with a product, you can send a message to the department. The department will then review your problem and send you a response by e-mail.

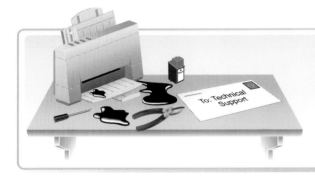

Share Your Knowledge

Many scientists and business professionals make their work available on the Web. If you are experienced in an area that many people are unfamiliar with, or if you have information that can help others, you can put the information on the Web.

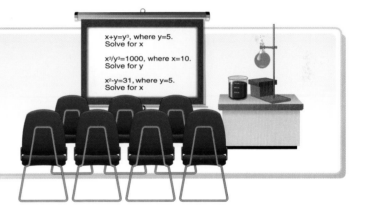

$x+y=y^3$, where $y=5$.
Solve for x

$x^3/y^3=1000$, where $x=10$.
Solve for y

$x^2-y=31$, where $y=5$.
Solve for x

Promote an Organization

You can use your Web pages to display information about an organization or club that you belong to. You can include detailed information about the goals of the organization and a schedule of upcoming events. Some services that make pages available on the Web let nonprofit organizations display their pages free of charge.

KNOW YOUR AUDIENCE

When designing Web pages, you must consider who will read the pages.

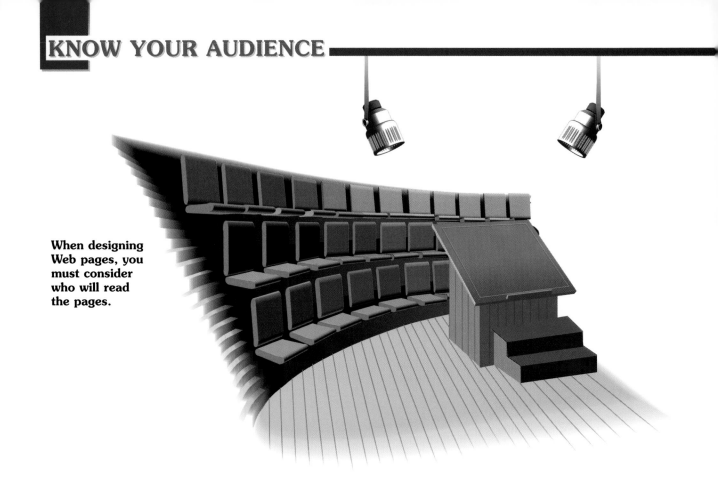

SPECIFIC AUDIENCE

You can design your Web pages to appeal to a specific audience. This will reduce the number of people who will visit your Web pages, but the people who do visit will be more likely to return on a regular basis. When designing Web pages for a specific audience, make sure you stick to the overall theme of your pages to maintain the interest of your readers.

GENERAL AUDIENCE

You can design your Web pages to appeal to a general audience. This will attract many visitors, but most of these people will only visit your pages once. When designing Web pages for a general audience, examine the available statistics about the people who use the Web.

WEB USER STATISTICS

These statistics were compiled by The Georgia Institute of Technology in January 1997. The latest statistics can be found at the following Web site:

http://www.cc.gatech.edu/gvu/user_surveys

Age

The average age of people who use the Web is about 35 years.

Gender

Over 68% of people who use the Web are male.

Income

The average household income of people who use the Web is $60,800 U.S.

Language

English is the primary language of 93% of people who use the Web.

Education

About 56% of people who use the Web have completed college or university.

Purpose

The most popular reasons for using the Web are browsing, entertainment, education and work.

STEPS FOR PUBLISHING WEB PAGES

Creating Web pages and then making them available on the World Wide Web is known as publishing. You must publish your pages before anyone can view them on the Web.

Plan Your Web Pages

Decide on a theme for your Web pages. If possible, try to make your theme unique. When planning your Web pages, first determine the goals you want the pages to accomplish and then plan the design of the pages.

Create the Text

Decide what information you want to present in your Web pages and then create the text. After you create the text, you can convert the text to HyperText Markup Language (HTML). HTML is the language used to display information on the Web.

Insert Links

A link allows readers to select an image or highlighted text to display another page on the Web. Links are one of the most important features of your Web pages since they let readers easily move through information of interest.

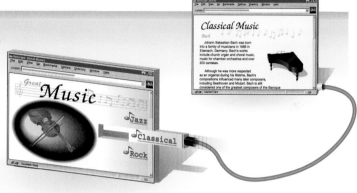

Insert Images

You can use images, such as pictures, logos or icons, to enhance the appearance of your Web pages. You can create these images on your computer, copy them from the Web or use a scanner to copy them from printed material.

Place Pages on the Web

When you finish creating your Web pages, you can transfer them to a service that makes pages available on the Web. Test your pages to ensure the information appears properly and all the links work. Then announce your Web pages to the world.

WEB PAGE CONTENT

There are many things you should consider when creating and maintaining Web pages. Following a few basic guidelines will help improve your Web pages.

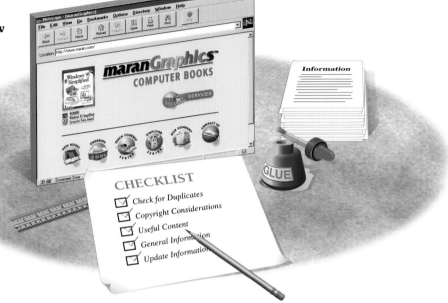

Check for Duplicates

Before you start putting your Web pages together, check to see if someone has already published Web pages containing the same information. Try to make your pages unique.

Copyright Considerations

If you are going to use information or an image from another source, make sure the information or image is not copyrighted. Many pages on the Web offer information and images that are free from copyright restrictions.

Put Useful Content on Each Page

Always include information that is valuable to the reader on each page. Even if you are designing a Web page that consists only of a table of contents, try to put some useful information on the page. This will give readers a reason to return to the Web page time and time again.

Provide General Information

Even if your Web pages are aimed at a specific audience, you should provide general background information. This ensures that any visitor to your Web pages will be able to fully understand the content of the pages you have published.

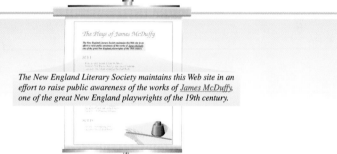

The New England Literary Society maintains this Web site in an effort to raise public awareness of the works of James McDuffy, one of the great New England playwrights of the 19th century.

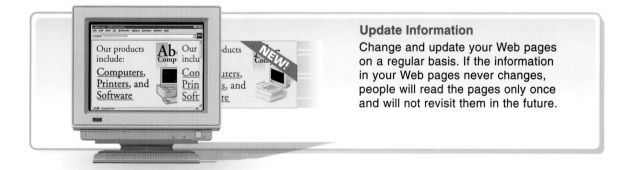

Update Information

Change and update your Web pages on a regular basis. If the information in your Web pages never changes, people will read the pages only once and will not revisit them in the future.

THE HOME PAGE

The home page is the main page in a collection of Web pages. The home page is usually the first page people read.

The home page is usually named **index.htm** or **index.html**

Use a Summary

Always place a brief summary of your Web pages on the home page. You should state whether the purpose of the Web pages is to amuse or inform readers. Never assume readers will understand what your pages are about just by reading the title.

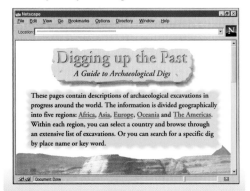

Table of Contents

Outline the contents of your Web pages on the home page. This allows readers to quickly find the information they want without having to read pages that do not interest them.

Remind Readers to Bookmark

The bookmark feature allows readers to mark Web pages for later reference. Most readers forget to use this Web browser feature, particularly if they are absorbed in reading the information on a page.

Include an image or phrase to remind readers to bookmark your page. The bookmark feature is also called a hotlist or favorites feature.

Include a Help Section

If you have a large collection of Web pages, you should include a help section on the home page. In the help section, explain which icons or navigational tools you will use on your Web pages.

Display Design Credits

If you are creating Web pages for other people, ask if you can put your name and e-mail address at the bottom of the home page. This will let readers know how to contact you if they have questions about the design or layout of the pages.

You can link text or images in your Web pages to related information on the Web. Linking is what makes the Web such a powerful tool.

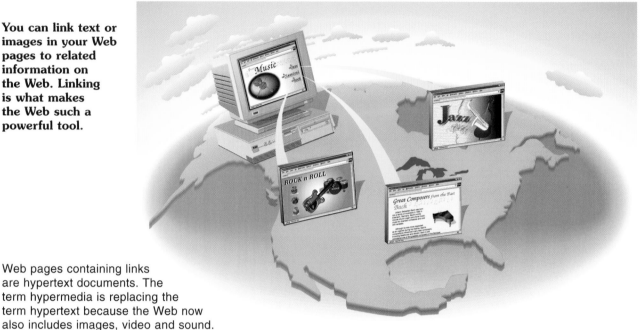

Web pages containing links are hypertext documents. The term hypermedia is replacing the term hypertext because the Web now also includes images, video and sound.

How Links Work

When viewing a Web page, readers can immediately view another Web page by selecting a link. A link will look different than the surrounding text or images. Most links let readers connect to other pages that relate to the page they are viewing.

URLs

Each page on the Web has a unique address. The address of each page is called the Uniform Resource Locator (URL). The URL for a Web page starts with http and contains the computer name, directory name and name of the Web page.

http://www.maran.com/books/95visual.html

REASONS FOR LINKS

Send E-Mail

Sometimes you will want readers to give you feedback. You can include a link on a Web page that lets readers send comments by e-mail.

Related Discussion Groups

A Web page can include a link to a discussion group, or newsgroup, that relates to the topic of your Web page.

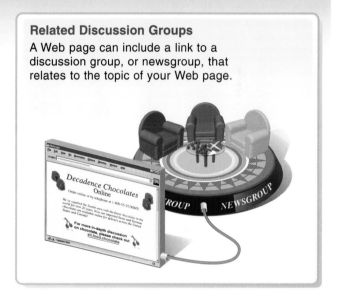

Get Files

File Transfer Protocol (FTP) sites allow readers to get files. You can use an FTP link to make software or information easily accessible to your readers.

Definitions

Definition links help readers who do not know the meaning of a word or phrase in your Web page. A definition link will take readers to a footnote or brief explanation.

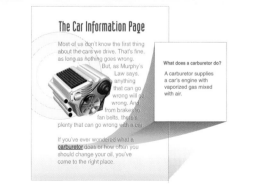

You can easily add an image to a Web page. An image that appears on a Web page is called an inline image.

Alternative Text

Some readers use Web browsers that cannot display images, while others turn off the display of images to browse more quickly. Since some readers may not see the images on your Web pages, you can specify the text you want to display instead of the images. This will help these readers know what they are missing.

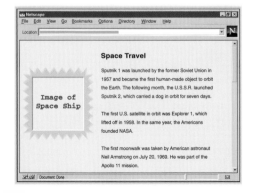

Background Images

You can have a small image repeat to fill an entire Web page. This can add an interesting background texture. Make sure the background image you choose does not affect the readability of your Web page.

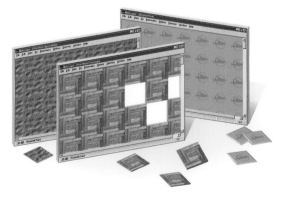

TYPES OF IMAGES

GIF

Graphics Interchange Format (GIF) images are the most common type of image found on the Web. GIF images are limited to 256 colors, which is the same number of colors most computer monitors can display. GIF is often used for logos, banners and computer-generated art. GIF images have the .gif extension.

JPEG

Joint Photographic Experts Group (JPEG) images are commonly found on the Web. JPEG images can have millions of colors and are often used for photographs and very complex images. JPEG images have the .jpg, .jpe or .jpeg extension.

PNG

Portable Network Graphics (PNG) images are a newer type of image specifically designed for use on the Web. PNG images can have millions of colors and will eventually replace GIF images. PNG images have the .png or .ping extension.

TABLES

Tables allow you to control the placement of text and images on your Web pages. Tables may seem complicated, but they are well worth learning how to create.

	Jan	Feb	March
Jason	435	726	988
Chris	658	589	697
Cathy	946	963	831
Peter	876	649	954

Table Elements

A table consists of rows, columns and cells.

Last Name	First Name	Street	City
Smith	John	258 Linton Ave.	New York
Lang	Kristin	50 Tree Lane	Boston
Oram	Derek	68 Cracker Ave.	San Francisco
Gray	Russell	401 Idon Dr.	Atlanta
Atherly	Peter	47 Crosby Ave.	Las Vegas
Talbot	Mark	26 Arnold Cres.	Greenwich

Row
A row is a horizontal line of data.

Column
A column is a vertical line of data.

Cell
A cell is the area where a row and column intersect.

Plan Ahead

Tables are often the most confusing part of learning HTML. The key to using tables is to plan the table before adding it to an HTML document. Always sketch your tables on paper before you begin.

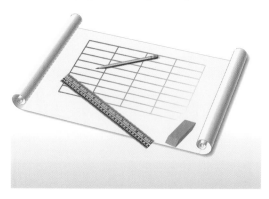

Lists of Information

Tables provide a great way to neatly present lists of information. You can use tables to display information such as financial data, telephone listings and price lists.

EMPLOYEE PHONE NUMBERS		
Name	**Department**	**Phone Number**
Allison, Steve	Accounting	555-1762
Atherly, Peter	Sales	555-2298
Boshart, Mark	Ordering	555-1270
Coleman, Dale	Sales	555-8851
Lang, Kristin	Shipping	555-9993
Lippert, Janet	Accounting	555-0042
Oram, Derek	Maintenance	555-7148
Sanvido, Dean	Service	555-0128
Smith, John	Sales	555-7018
Talbot, Mark	Ordering	555-1510

Newspaper-Style Columns

You can use tables to present information in newspaper-style columns. You can make a table without borders so the structure of the table is invisible. To create a Web page with three newspaper-style columns, place your text in a table containing one row with three cells.

Borders

You can use a table to place a three-dimensional border around text or an image. A border will make text or an image appear raised above your Web page. To place a border around text or an image, place the text or image in a table containing one row with one cell.

TRANSFER FILES TO WEB PRESENCE PROVIDER

A Web presence provider is a company that can store your Web pages on a computer called a Web server. Once the files are on the Web server, your Web pages will be available to everyone on the Web.

Most Internet service providers and commercial online services are also Web presence providers.

File Names

Some Web presence providers may not accept file names beyond a certain length or file names that include spaces or unusual characters.

Make sure all your files have an extension to indicate the type of file. Web pages have the .html or .htm extension.

Check File Permissions

Some Web presence providers restrict access to Web pages. If you receive a "Permission Error" when you try to access your Web pages, contact the presence provider to find out how to change the file permissions.

Keep Organized

Find out the name of the directory that will store your files. Most Web servers will store your files in a directory named **public_html**

If you have a small number of files, you can place all the files in the public_html directory. If you have a large number of files, you can use subdirectories, or folders, to organize your files.

Check Links

If you place files in different directories, carefully check the links that connect your Web pages to ensure the links still work.

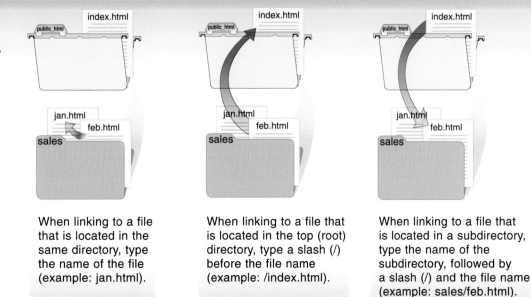

When linking to a file that is located in the same directory, type the name of the file (example: jan.html).

When linking to a file that is located in the top (root) directory, type a slash (/) before the file name (example: /index.html).

When linking to a file that is located in a subdirectory, type the name of the subdirectory, followed by a slash (/) and the file name (example: sales/feb.html).

TEST YOUR WEB PAGES

You should carefully test your Web pages to make sure they look and work the way you planned. Many readers will not return to Web pages containing errors.

Check Spelling
Check the spelling on each of your Web pages before making them available on the Web. Spelling errors will make readers question the amount of effort you put into creating your Web pages.

The following Web site will check your pages for spelling errors:

http://www2.imagiware.com/RxHTML

Use a Validation Service
Use a validation service on the Web to check all of your Web pages for errors. A validation service will visit your Web pages and notify you of any errors in your use of HTML.

One of the most popular validation services is WebTechs, located at:

http://www.webtechs.com

Test Presentation

You should test your Web pages to see how easily you can access and browse through the information.

Ensure the Web pages have a consistent design and writing style and also check for formatting and layout errors.

Verify Links

Check all the links in your Web pages to make sure the links take you to the intended destinations. Regularly check links to pages you did not create. This lets you ensure the linked pages still exist and contain information of interest to your readers.

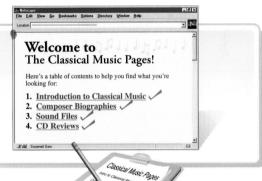

Use a Test Audience

Ask your friends, family members and colleagues with little Web browsing experience to check out your Web pages.

Ask their opinions on the content and design of your Web pages. Compare their comments to a list of your objectives to determine which areas still need work.

PUBLICIZE YOUR WEB PAGES

Once your pages are available on the Web, you need to let the world know about the pages. There is no central location where you can publicize your Web pages, so you must use several methods.

Exchange Links

If another page on the Web discusses ideas related to your Web page, ask if they will include a link to your page if you do the same. This way, people reading the other page can easily visit your page.

Web Page Banners

Many companies set aside areas on their Web pages where you can advertise your pages. The Internet Link Exchange helps you advertise your Web pages free of charge. The Internet Link Exchange is located at:

http://www.linkexchange.com

Search Tools

You can have your Web pages added to the catalogs of various search tools on the Web. Search tools help people search for a specific topic or browse through categories to find Web pages of interest.

WebStep TOP 100 provides descriptions of the top 100 search tools on the Web. You can add your Web pages to the search tools that best fit your audience. You can find WebStep at:

http://www.mmgco.com/top100.html

Submit It! lets you add your Web pages to many search tools at one time. Submit It! is located at:

http://www.submit-it.com

Newsgroups

You can send an announcement of your Web pages to carefully selected discussion groups, called newsgroups. Each newsgroup on the Internet discusses a particular topic.

Read the articles in a newsgroup for a week before sending an announcement. This lets you make sure the topics discussed relate to your Web pages. Sending an announcement to inappropriate newsgroups is called spamming and is not approved of on the Internet.

The following newsgroup lets you announce new or updated Web pages:

comp.infosystems.www.announce

GREAT WEB SITES

You can browse through these Web sites to get ideas for your own Web pages.

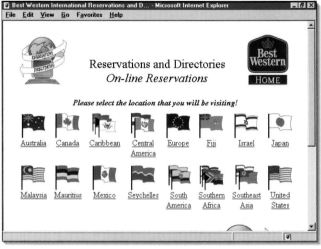

Best Western International
URL http://www.bestwestern.com

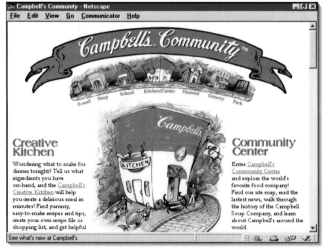

Campbell Soup Company
URL http://www.campbellsoup.com

CNET: The Computer Network
URL http://www.cnet.com

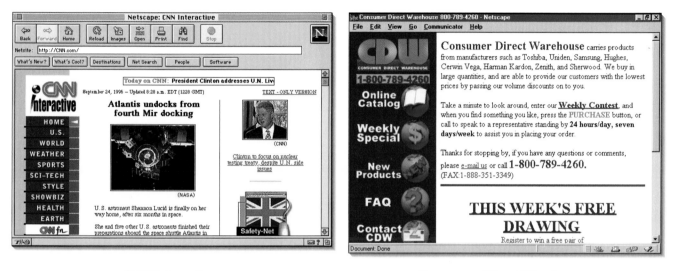

CNN Interactive

URL http://www.cnn.com

Consumer Direct Warehouse

URL http://consumer-direct.com

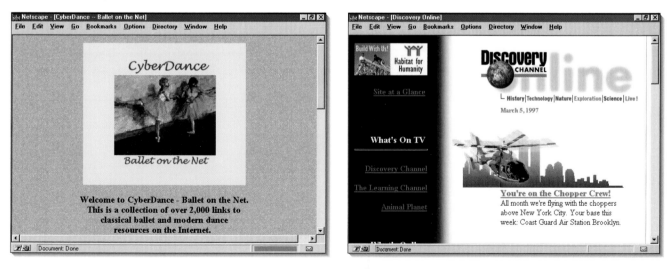

CyberDance

URL http://www.thepoint.net/~raw/dance.htm

Discovery Channel Online

URL http://www.discovery.com

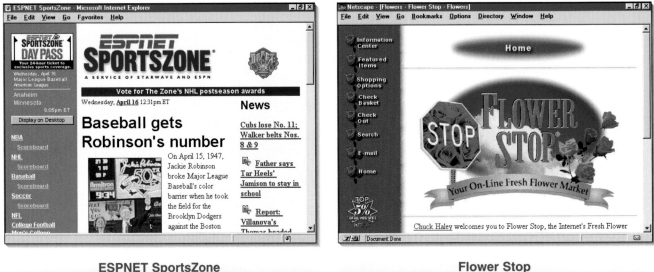

ESPNET SportsZone
URL http://espnet.sportszone.com

Flower Stop
URL http://www.flowerstop.com

golf.com
URL http://www.golf.com

Hotels and Travel on the Net
URL http://www.hotelstravel.com

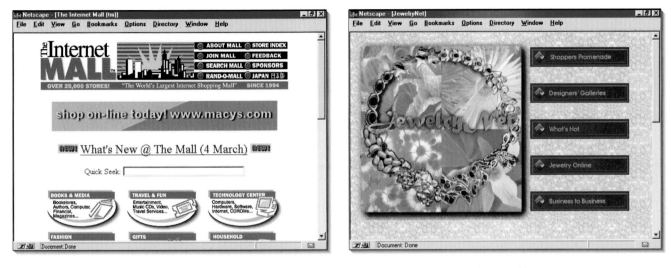

Internet Mall

 http://www.internet-mall.com

JewelryNet

 http://www.jewelrynet.com

Lycos

 http://www.lycos.com

MovieWEB

 http://movieweb.com/movie/movie.html

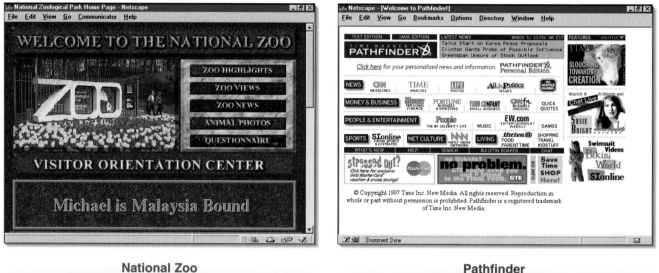

National Zoo
URL http://www.si.edu/natzoo

Pathfinder
URL http://www.pathfinder.com

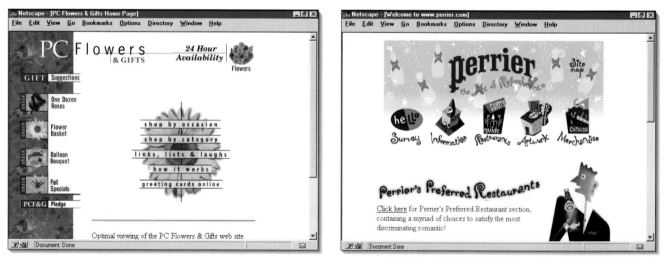

PC Flowers & Gifts
URL http://www.pcflowers.com

Perrier
URL http://www.perrier.com

Smithsonian Institution
URL http://www.si.edu

Spiegel
URL http://www.spiegel.com

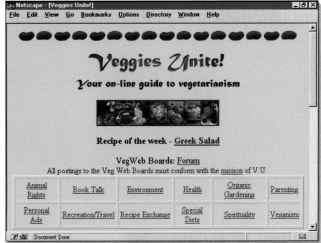

USA Today
URL http://www.usatoday.com

Veggies Unite!
URL http://vegweb.com

judy@abc.com

28.8 Fax modem

Electronic Mail

What is electronic mail? Find out in this chapter how the Internet's most popular feature lets you communicate with people around the world.

INTRODUCTION TO E-MAIL

You can exchange electronic mail (e-mail) with people around the world.

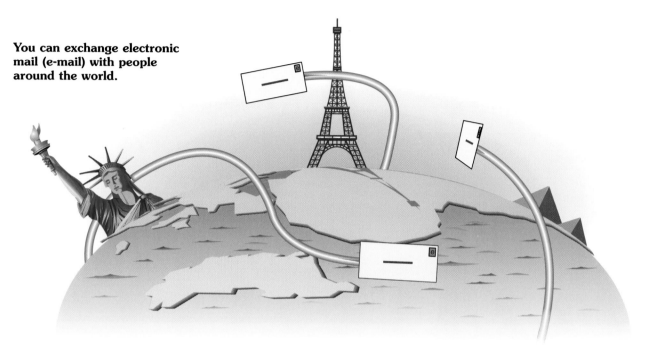

E-mail provides a fast, economical and convenient way to send messages to family, friends and colleagues.

Speed

E-mail is much faster than old-fashioned mail, called "snail mail." An e-mail message can travel around the world in seconds.

Cost

Once you pay a service provider for a connection to the Internet, there is no charge for sending and receiving e-mail. You do not have to pay extra even if you send a long message or the message travels around the world.

Exchanging e-mail can save you money on long-distance calls. The next time you are about to pick up the telephone, consider sending an e-mail message instead.

Convenience

You can compose and send e-mail messages whenever it is convenient for you. Unlike telephone calls, e-mail messages do not require the recipient to be there when you send a message. E-mail makes communicating with people in different time zones very convenient.

Transfer Files

You can use e-mail to get files from the Internet. Some computers on the Internet store large collections of files. You can send an e-mail message to one of these computers and the computer will automatically transfer the file you requested to your computer.

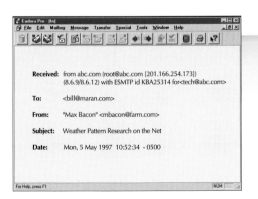

Headers

Every e-mail message contains information called a header. When you display the header for an e-mail message, you can view information about the person who sent the message, the date and time the message was sent and even a list of all the computers on the Internet the message passed through before reaching your computer.

E-MAIL PROGRAMS

An e-mail program lets you send, receive and manage your e-mail messages.

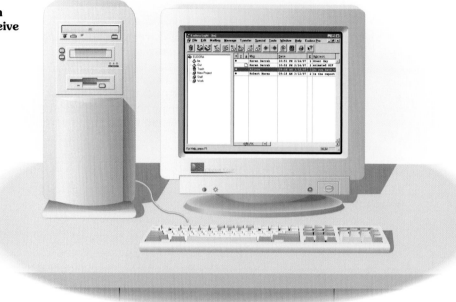

POPULAR E-MAIL PROGRAMS

Popular e-mail programs include Eudora Light and Netscape Mail.

Eudora Light
■ This area displays a list of all the e-mail messages.

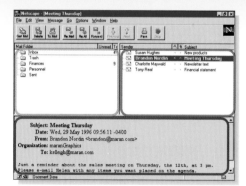

Netscape Mail
■ This area displays the folders that contain your e-mail messages.

■ This area displays a list of all the e-mail messages.

■ This area displays the contents of a single e-mail message.

E-MAIL PROGRAM FEATURES

Organization

E-mail programs usually store messages you have sent, received and deleted in separate folders. This helps you keep messages organized so you can review them later. You can also create personalized folders to better organize your messages.

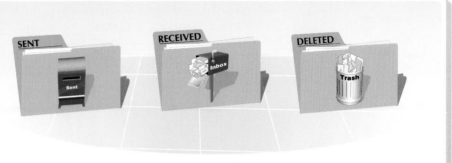

Filters

Some e-mail programs can automatically sort your e-mail messages into folders for you. This is called filtering.

You can create a simple filter to have the e-mail program place all messages from a certain person in one folder.

Spell Checking

Most e-mail programs now come with a spell checking feature. Before you send a message, the spell checker compares every word in the message to words in its dictionary.

If a word does not exist in the dictionary, the spell checker considers the word misspelled. The spell checker will ask if you want to change the spelling of the word and may suggest a replacement.

E-MAIL ADDRESSES

You can send a message to anyone around the world if you know the person's e-mail address.

An e-mail address defines the location of an individual's mailbox on the Internet.

Parts of an E-Mail Address

An e-mail address consists of two parts separated by the @ (at) symbol. An e-mail address cannot contain spaces.

max@company.com

■ The **user name** is the name of the person's account. This can be a real name or a nickname.

■ The **domain name** is the location of the person's account on the Internet. Periods (.) separate the various parts of the domain name.

Famous E-Mail Addresses

FAMOUS

NAME	ADDRESS
Bill Gates	billg@microsoft.com
Brad Pitt	ciaobox@msn.com
Madonna	Madonna@wbr.com
U.S. President	president@whitehouse.gov
Tom Brokaw	nightly@nbc.com
Tom Clancy	tomclancy@aol.com

Organization or Country

The last few characters in an e-mail address usually indicate the type of organization or country to which the person belongs.

ORGANIZATION

com	commercial
edu	education
gov	government
mil	military
net	network
org	organization (often non-profit)

COUNTRY

au	Australia
ca	Canada
it	Italy
jp	Japan
uk	United Kingdom

Bounced Messages

A bounced message is a message that returns to you because it cannot reach its destination. A message usually bounces because of typing mistakes in the e-mail address.

Before sending a message, make sure you check the e-mail address for accuracy.

Wrong Address

Writing Style

Make sure every message you send is clear, concise and contains no spelling or grammar errors. Also make sure the message will not be misinterpreted. For example, the reader may not realize a statement is meant to be sarcastic.

Smileys

You can use special characters, called smileys or emoticons, to express emotions in messages. The characters resemble human faces if you turn them sideways.

SMILEYS

Gesture	Characters
Cry	:'-(
Frown	:-(
Indifferent	:-I
Laugh	:-D
Smile	:-)
Surprise	:-0
Wink	;-)

Abbreviations

Abbreviations are commonly used in messages to save time typing.

Abbreviation	Meaning	Abbreviation	Meaning
BTW	by the way	LOL	laughing out loud
FAQ	frequently asked questions	MOTAS	member of the appropriate sex
FOAF	friend of a friend	MOTOS	member of the opposite sex
FWIW	for what it's worth		
FYI	for your information	MOTSS	member of the same sex
IMHO	in my humble opinion		
IMO	in my opinion	ROTFL	rolling on the floor laughing
IOW	in other words	SO	significant other
L8R	later	WRT	with respect to

Shouting

A MESSAGE WRITTEN
IN CAPITAL LETTERS IS
ANNOYING AND HARD
TO READ. THIS IS
CALLED SHOUTING.

Always use upper
and lower case letters
when typing messages.

Flame

A flame is an angry or
insulting message directed
at one person. A flame
war is an argument that
continues for a while.

Avoid starting
or participating
in flame wars.

Signature

You can have an e-mail
program add information
about yourself to the end
of every message you send.
This prevents you from
having to type the same
information over and over
again.

A signature can include your
name, e-mail address, occupation
or favorite quotation. You can also
use plain characters to display
simple pictures. Do not create a
signature that is more than four
lines long.

From:
Address of the person
sending the message.

To:
Address of the person
receiving the message.

From:	mary@sales.abc.com
To:	john@sales.abc.com
Subject:	Sales Awards
Cc:	sarah@sales.abc.com
Bcc:	karen@abc.com

Congratulations on your achievement!
I'm looking forward to seeing you at the
awards ceremony!

Subject:
Identifies the contents of
the message. Make sure
your subject is informative.
Do not use subjects such
as "For your information"
or "Read this now."

Cc:
Stands for "carbon copy." A carbon
copy is an exact copy of a message.
You can send a carbon copy of a
message to a person who is not
directly involved but would be
interested in the message.

Bcc:
Stands for "blind carbon copy."
This lets you send the same
message to several people
without them knowing that
others have also received
the same message.

ATTACH A FILE TO A MESSAGE

You can attach a document, picture, sound, video or program to a message you are sending.

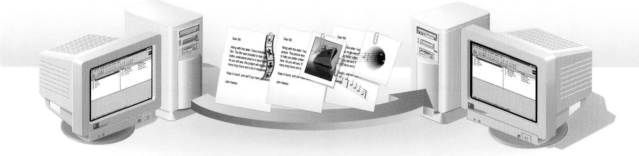

Many e-mail programs use Multipurpose Internet Mail Extensions (MIME) to attach files to messages.

To view an attached file, the computer receiving the message must be able to understand MIME. The computer must also have a program that can view or play the file.

COMPRESS ATTACHED FILES

When you want to attach a large file to an e-mail message, you can save time and money by compressing the file. Compressing a file shrinks the file to a smaller size. This allows the file to transfer more quickly over the Internet.

You can also use a compression program to combine numerous files into a single file. This means you do not need to attach each file individually to an e-mail message.

The person receiving a compressed file must use a decompression program to expand the file to its original form.

You can send a message to exchange ideas or request information.

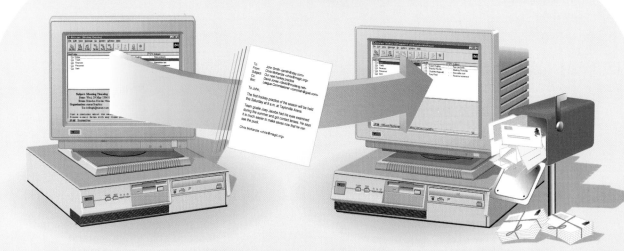

If you want to practice sending a message, send a message to yourself.

When you send a message, do not assume the person will read the message right away. Some people do not regularly check their messages.

Compose Offline

You can write e-mail messages when you are not connected to the Internet (offline). When you finish writing all your messages, you can connect and send all the messages at once. If you have to pay for the time you spend online, composing messages offline will save you money.

Use the Address Book

An e-mail program provides an address book where you can store the addresses of people you frequently send messages to. An address book saves you from having to type the same addresses over and over again.

Send a Message to Many Addresses

You can send a message to many e-mail addresses at once. To do so, you must first assign a name to a group of e-mail addresses.

When you send a message to the name you assigned to the group, the message will be sent to every e-mail address in the group. This feature is useful if you want to send announcements or newsletters to everyone on a mailing list.

Send Several Messages at Once

E-mail messages can often take a while to transfer from your computer. This can slow down your connection to the Internet and prevent you from performing other tasks, such as browsing the Web. If you need to send several messages, you can use your time more efficiently by sending all the messages at once.

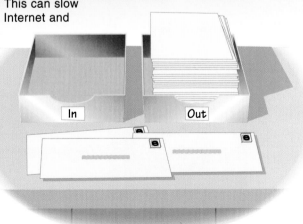

When you finish typing each message, you can place the message in a special folder and then send all the messages in the folder at a convenient time.

Receive Messages

Your Internet access provider stores messages you receive in a mailbox for you. When you check for new messages, you are checking your mailbox on the access provider's computer.

Check for new messages on a regular basis. If your mailbox gets too full, your access provider may delete some of your messages.

You can use most computers with a modem to connect to your access provider and retrieve messages. This allows you to check your messages while traveling.

Automatically Check for Messages

Most e-mail programs automatically check for new e-mail messages. You can specify how often you want the program to check for new messages.

You should have the e-mail program check for messages approximately every 30 minutes. If your e-mail program is constantly checking for new messages, it can slow down the performance of other tasks, such as browsing the Web.

Reply to a Message

You can reply to a message to answer a question, express an opinion or supply additional information.

When you reply to a message, make sure you include part of the original message. This is called quoting. Quoting helps the reader identify which message you are replying to. To save the reader time, make sure you delete all parts of the original message that do not directly relate to your reply.

Forward a Message

After reading a message, you can add comments and then send the message to a friend or colleague.

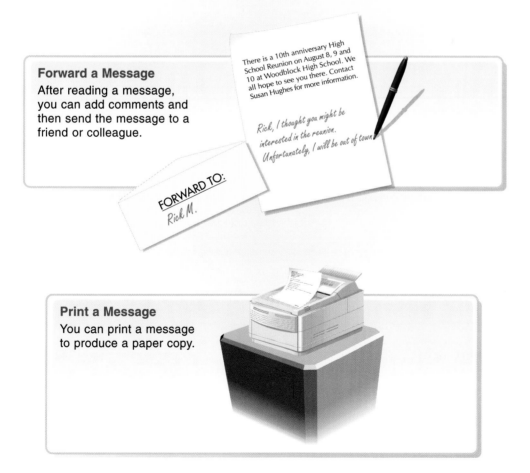

Print a Message

You can print a message to produce a paper copy.

CHILDREN AND E-MAIL

E-mail is often the easiest way for children to get started using the Internet. You should carefully monitor the e-mail messages your children send and receive.

Adult Supervision

Constant adult supervision is the best way to ensure that children are not communicating with strangers by e-mail. Check every e-mail message your children send or receive to make sure they are not communicating with people you are not aware of.

Set Guidelines

Before letting your children use e-mail, discuss which types of information are acceptable and which types of information to be wary of. Many countries around the world have access to the Internet. Information that is considered acceptable in one country may be inappropriate where you live. Children should tell a parent or other adult if they do not feel comfortable about any e-mail messages they receive.

Limit E-Mail Messages

Many schools now allow students to use the computers at school to send and receive e-mail messages.

You can restrict your children to exchanging e-mail with their friends and other children they have met at school.

Personal Information

Children should never reveal personal information about themselves, such as which school they attend or where they live.

Children should also never mention the location of any clubs or organizations they participate in. Most organizations do not have a security policy and may reveal your address to anyone who contacts the organization.

Family Web Pages

Many families have their own pages on the World Wide Web. Many of these pages allow readers to send e-mail messages to members of the family.

You should not display your phone number, address or any pictures of your children on your family Web pages.

FIND E-MAIL ADDRESSES WITH FOUR11

Four11 has over 6 million e-mail addresses in their database. If you do not know the e-mail address of someone you want to send a message to, you can search for the address in Four11.

E-Mail Listings

You can search the Four11 database by entering a few details about the person you want to find, such as first name, last name and geographic location. The more information you enter, the better the results of the search will be.

Sleeper Searches

If you cannot find the person you are looking for, you can have Four11 perform a Sleeper Search. Four11 will continue checking the e-mail database at regular intervals and will notify you when the person is found. This feature is very useful if the person you are looking for has not yet joined the Internet but will join in the future.

Telephone Listings

You can use Four11 to search for the telephone number of anyone in the United States. You can enter a name and any part of the address for the person you want to find.

Four11 will display the person's telephone number and e-mail address, if it is available.

Government Listings

Four11 includes a directory of United States government officials. The directory includes information on federal and state governments as well as various committees.

You can use the directory to find out how to contact the government officials for your area.

Internet Phone Listings

Four11 contains a directory of people who use their computers as voice or video phones to communicate over the Internet. If you want to communicate with another person using an Internet phone, you must both use the same type of Internet phone software.

You can search Four11 to find people using the same type of software that you use.

SEND ANONYMOUS E-MAIL

You can send an e-mail message to anyone on the Internet without revealing your identity.

You can use one of the following services to send e-mail anonymously:

http://www.cs.berkeley.edu/~raph/n.a.n.html

http://remailer.nl.com/~remailer

Reasons for Anonymous E-Mail

You can send anonymous e-mail messages to individuals, mailing lists and newsgroups on the Internet. This is very useful because many newsgroups and mailing lists are for support groups whose members want to remain unknown.

Send Anonymous E-Mail

When you use an anonymous mailing service, a computer called an anonymous remailer removes your name and e-mail address from the message and replaces the information with an identification number.

People can reply to your messages by sending the reply to the anonymous remailer. The remailer then forwards the reply to your computer.

Finger is a program that lets you learn more about a person on the Internet. You can also use a finger program to find out who is currently using a computer connected to the Internet.

Sue Smith
ssmith@web.com
(555) 555-1234

Kevin Inglis
kinglis@abc.com
(555) 555-2301

Bob King
bob@maran.com
(555) 555-5475

You can use finger on the World Wide Web at:

http://www.populus.net/cgi-bin/HyperFinger

Information

When you finger a person's e-mail address, you can display a variety of information about the person. You can often view the person's real name and telephone number or a message written by the person.

Check with your Internet access provider to find out if you can set up the information that will appear when people finger your e-mail address.

dsmith@abc.com
(555) 555-2409

I'm on vacation from May 16th to June 5th and will not be checking my e-mail messages.

Finger Services

You can finger the following e-mail addresses to view interesting information:

quake@geophys.washington.edu

nasanews@space.mit.edu

help@dir.su.oz.au

Mailing Lists

What are mailing lists and how do they work? This chapter introduces you to mailing lists and provides a selection of interesting mailing lists you can join.

INTRODUCTION TO MAILING LISTS

A mailing list is a discussion group that uses e-mail to communicate.

There are thousands of mailing lists that cover a wide variety of topics, from aromatherapy to ZZTop. New mailing lists are created every week.

How Mailing Lists Work

When a mailing list receives a message, a copy of the message goes to everyone on the mailing list.

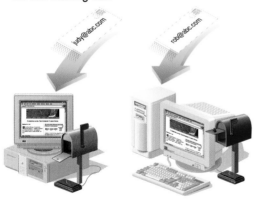

Most mailing lists let you send and receive messages. Some mailing lists only let you receive messages.

Find Mailing Lists

You can find an index of mailing lists at the following Web site:

http://www.neosoft.com/internet/paml

You can search for mailing lists that discuss a specific topic at the following Web site:

http://www.liszt.com

Cost

You can join most mailing lists free of charge. Mailing lists that charge people to join are usually used for distributing newsletters and electronic news such as stock market figures.

Start a Mailing List

You can easily start your own mailing list. If only a few people will be using the list, you can run the list with a regular e-mail program on your own computer. Most Internet access providers have programs dedicated to running large mailing lists for their customers. Running your own mailing list can be very time consuming.

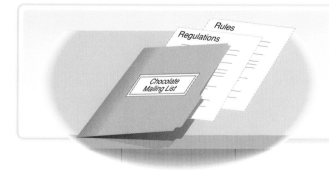

Get Information

Before you join a mailing list, try to get as much information as possible about the list. Most mailing lists have their own rules and regulations. Mailing lists often provide an e-mail address where you can send a message to request information about the list.

SUBSCRIBE TO A MAILING LIST

Just as you would subscribe to a newspaper or magazine, you can subscribe to a mailing list that interests you.

Subscribing adds your e-mail address to the mailing list.

Mailing List
Subscribe Here!
chris@xyz.com
ben@bookstore.com
carl@sales.abc.com
david@maran.com
jack@123.com

e-mail addresses
andrew@iog.com
christie@mss.com
julie@bcb.com
noel@cyber.com
tamara@vox.com
russ@wav.com
susan@123.com

Unsubscribe

If you no longer want to receive messages from a mailing list, you can unsubscribe from the mailing list at any time. Unsubscribing removes your e-mail address from the mailing list.

MAILING LIST ADDRESSES

Each mailing list has two addresses. Make sure you send your messages to the appropriate address.

Mailing List Address

The mailing list address receives messages intended for the entire mailing list. This is the address you use to send messages you want all the people on the list to receive. Do not send subscription or unsubscription requests to the mailing list address.

Administrative Address

The administrative address receives messages dealing with administrative issues. This is the address you use to subscribe to or unsubscribe from a mailing list.

Mailing List

Administrative

NA-Soccer   Ghost Stories

SUBSCRIBE
☐ A.Word.A.Day
☐ Choco
☐ Melrose Place

Welcome Message

When you subscribe to a mailing list, you will receive a welcome message to confirm that your e-mail address has been added to the list. This message will also explain any rules the mailing list has about sending messages to the list.

Check for Messages

After you subscribe to a mailing list, make sure you check your mailbox frequently. You can receive dozens of messages in a short period of time.

Digests

If you receive a lot of messages from a mailing list, find out if the list is available as a digest. A digest groups individual messages together and sends them to you as one message.

Vacations

When you go on vacation, make sure you temporarily unsubscribe from all your mailing lists. This will prevent your mailbox from overflowing with messages.

TYPES OF MAILING LISTS

Manually Maintained Lists

A person manages a manually maintained mailing list.

A manually maintained list usually contains the word "request" in its e-mail address (example: hang-gliding-request@lists.utah.edu).

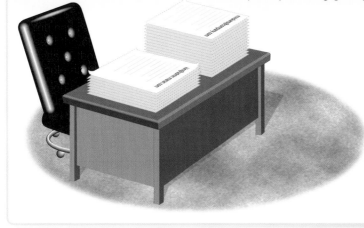

Join a List

When you want to join a manually maintained list, make sure you find out what information the administrator needs and include the information in your message.

Automated Lists

A computer program manages an automated mailing list. There are three popular programs that manage automated lists—listproc, listserv and majordomo.

An automated list typically contains the name of the program that manages the list in its e-mail address (example: listserv@ubvm.cc.buffalo.edu).

Join a List

When you want to join an automated list, make sure you find out what information the program needs and include the information in your message. If a program does not understand your message, it may not respond to your request.

MAILING LIST RESTRICTIONS

Restricted Mailing Lists

Some mailing lists restrict the number of people allowed to join the list. If you want to join one of these lists, you may have to wait for someone else to leave the list.

Other mailing lists require that you meet certain qualifications to join the list. For example, a mailing list about surgery may be restricted to medical doctors.

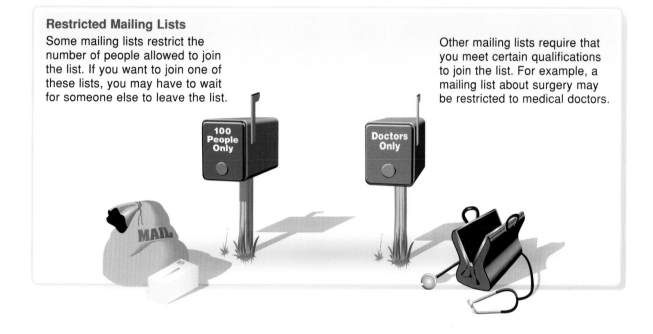

Moderated Mailing Lists

Some mailing lists are moderated. A volunteer reads each message sent to a moderated list and decides if the message is appropriate for the list. If the message is appropriate, the volunteer sends the message to every person on the mailing list.

A moderated mailing list keeps discussions on topic and removes messages containing ideas already discussed.

In an unmoderated mailing list, all messages are automatically sent to everyone on the list.

MAILING LIST ETIQUETTE

Mailing list etiquette refers to the proper way to behave when sending messages to a mailing list.

Read the messages in a mailing list for a week before sending a message. This is a good way to learn how people in a mailing list communicate and prevents you from submitting inappropriate information or information already discussed.

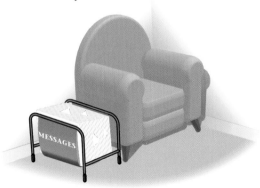

Hundreds of people may read a message you send to a mailing list. Before sending a message, make sure you carefully reread the message.

Make sure your message is clear, concise and contains no spelling or grammar errors.

Also make sure your message will not be misinterpreted. For example, not all readers will realize a statement is meant to be sarcastic.

MESSAGE

I found a flower in my bakyard and I want to identify it. It's sort of tall, colored blue and purple, maybe with red dots on it's leaves. If anyone can help me, I'd appreciate it.

○ -Spelling mistakes
? -Unclear

SUBJECT

The subject of a message is the first item people read. Make sure the subject clearly identifies the contents of the message. For example, the subject "Read this now" or "For your information" is not very informative.

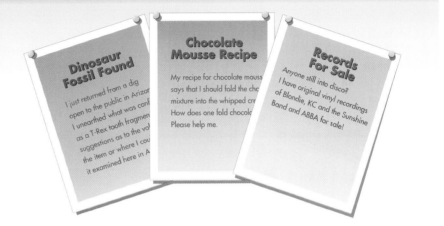

Dinosaur Fossil Found

I just returned from a dig open to the public in Arizon I unearthed what was conf as a T-Rex tooth fragmen suggestions as to the va the item or where I cou it examined here in A

Chocolate Mousse Recipe

My recipe for chocolate mouss says that I should fold the cho mixture into the whipped cr How does one fold chocol Please help me.

Records For Sale

Anyone still into disco? I have original vinyl recordings of Blondie, KC and the Sunshine Band and ABBA for sale!

REPLY TO MESSAGES

You can reply to a message to answer a question, express an opinion or supply additional information. Reply to a message only when you have something important to say. A reply such as "Me too" or "I agree" is not very useful.

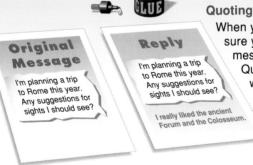

Original Message

I'm planning a trip to Rome this year. Any suggestions for sights I should see?

Reply

I'm planning a trip to Rome this year. Any suggestions for sights I should see?

I really liked the ancient Forum and the Colosseum.

Quoting

When you reply to a message, make sure you include some of the original message. This is called quoting. Quoting helps readers identify which message you are replying to. To save readers time, make sure you delete all parts of the original message that do not directly relate to your reply.

Private Replies

If your reply would not be of interest to others in a mailing list or if you want to send a private response, send a message to the author instead of sending your reply to the entire mailing list.

INTERESTING MAILING LISTS

2000ad-l
Discussion of the millennial year 2000.
Contact: listproc@usc.edu

Type in message:
subscribe 2000ad-l *Your Name*

Dinosaur
Discussion of dinosaurs and other prehistoric animals.
Contact: listproc@usc.edu

Type in message:
subscribe dinosaur *Your Name*

A.Word.A.Day
Sends you a word and its definition every day.
Contact: wsmith@wordsmith.org

Type in subject line:
subscribe *Your Name*

Ghost Stories
Ghost stories and other spooky discussions.
Contact: ghost-stories-request@
　　　　aurora.cdb.com

Choco
Sends you a collection of chocolate recipes once a month.
Contact: majordomo@apk.net

Type in message:
subscribe choco

Homebrew
Discussion of beer and other fermented beverages.
Contact: homebrew-request@
　　　　hpfcmi.fc.hp.com

Type in message:
subscribe

Diabetic
Where diabetics can exchange ideas and comments.
Contact: listserv@lehigh.edu

Type in message:
subscribe diabetic *Your Name*

Kidsbooks
Reviews of children's books.
Contact: kidsbooks-request@
　　　　armory.com

Melrose Place

Discussion of the popular television series.
Contact: majordomo@tcp.com

Type in message:
subscribe melrose-place

Pen Pals

A place for children to correspond on the Internet.
Contact: pen-pals-request
@mainstream.com

Movie Review

A resource for movie reviews.
Contact: moviereview–request@
cuenet.com

Type in message:
subscribe

Tennis Server Interactive

Monthly tennis news, tips and notices.
Contact: racquet-notices-request
@tennisserver.com

NA–Soccer

Discussion of North American soccer.
Contact: majordomo@hoplite.org

Type in message:
subscribe na–soccer

Veggie

Discussion of issues relevant to vegetarians.
Contact: veggie-request@
maths.bath.ac.uk

Offroad

Information and discussions about 4x4 and offroad driving.
Contact: offroad-request@
off-road.com

Weights

Discussion of all aspects of weightlifting.
Contact: weights-request@
fa.disney.com

EXAMINER

$ .75
Section A
Monday December 22, 1997

K12
Most School Kids Surf the Net
By Tina Veltri

The results of a recent survey show that 65 per cent of North American elementary school children know how to use the Internet.

"Most schools are incorporating computer-based learning in the classrooms," stated Jason Marcuson, head of the Social Survey Statisticians Group.

According to Marcuson, even children in Grades 1 and 2 had some type of Internet knowledge. "Most of these kids have a computer at home, so they've had exposure to the World Wide Web," said Marcuson.

The survey indicates that children in the '90s are more likely to pursue information-based careers. Marcuson says that high school administrators should pay careful attention to the results of this survey.

"Secondary school administrators should be planning to implement various computer courses into their curriculums," stated Marcuson, "in order to prepare their graduates for post-secondary programs in the technological field.

Marcuson further stated that the survey might be a hot topic of discussion at a number of elementary school board meetings. According to Marcuson, some schools don't have the finances that are needed in order to purchase computer equipment. However, once administrators realize the importance of computer-based learning, the schools will find ways to come up with the funds.

"We're living in a technologically advanced society, and kids will be at a disadvantage if they're not exposed to the Internet," stated Marcuson.

Soc Newsgro
People Waiting Longer to Tie the Knot
By Michael Wolfe

Studies have shown that North American couples are waiting longer to get married.

Ron Ratoff, professor of Sociology at Sir Peter University in Michigan, stated that this trend is explained by the rise in university enrollment.

"More people are getting a university education," said Ratoff, "so we're seeing less people settling down in their early 20s."

According to Ratoff, many people used to finish high school and head straight into the work force. Therefore, they married at an earlier age. But, today's high

dema
educa
stayin
ultima
Ratof
intere
which

Comp — Bubble Jets vs. Laser Printers
By Peter Lejcar

When deciding what type of printer to buy, most often the question is whether to buy an ink/bubble jet printer or a laser printer. At best, this topic is confusing enough, what with all the different makes and types on the market today. That's not to mention the fairly even popularity each type share. Ask your friends or neighbors which kind of printer they prefer and you can bet on a 50/50 split.

Most often, the tendency to buy one type of printer over the other is affected by personal preference, a sound investigation into each type of printer and its features, or the advice of others who already favor the printer that they own. For those of you who feel the urge to purchase the printer that your fellow computer buff has bought, delay your trip to the computer store. This article may shed some light on printer selection based on your needs and most importantly, your budget.

Perhaps the most important criterion for clearly distinguishing the laser printer from the bubble jet printer is the print quality. There is no question that a laser jet can produce a higher print quality than a standard bubble jet, but costs can be drastically reduced if you're willing to settle for a near-to-laser quality. Some bubble jet printers are known to compete with laser printers in this

respe
consu
of bu
marke
their r
Color
impor

Biz — Business in the New Millennium
By Brenda Petterson

The National Institute for Business in the New Millennium introduces a new publication, designed to aid you in understanding and implementing environmental management system that complies with the ISO 14001 standard, and monitor your progress. Included in this publication are complete steps

Mike Oliver, chairperson of Meko Inc., stated "This is such an informative book, the improvements were easy to incorporate and integrated well

More

g Days

stmas!

secondary
people are
ger, and
e.
is is an
cal study
at will

aiting, E3

p to the
the types
le on the
alities that
nise.
issue of

inters, B5

Newsgroups

What are newsgroups and what are the main categories of newsgroups? In this chapter you will learn how newsgroups allow people around the world with common interests to communicate with each other.

INTRODUCTION TO NEWSGROUPS

A newsgroup is a discussion group that allows people with common interests to communicate with each other.

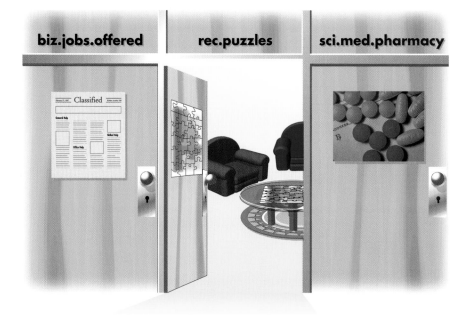

biz.jobs.offered   rec.puzzles   sci.med.pharmacy

There are thousands of newsgroups on every subject imaginable. Each newsgroup discusses a particular topic such as jobs offered, puzzles or medicine.

Usenet, short for Users' Network, refers to all the computers that are connected to distribute newsgroup information.

NEWSGROUP NAMES

The name of a newsgroup describes the type of information discussed in the newsgroup. A newsgroup name consists of two or more words, separated by periods (.).

The first word describes the main topic (example: **rec** for recreation). Each of the following words narrows the topic.

rec.sport.basketball.pro

ARTICLES

A newsgroup can contain hundreds or thousands of articles.

Article

An article is a message an individual posts, or sends, to a newsgroup. An article can be a few lines of text or the length of a book.

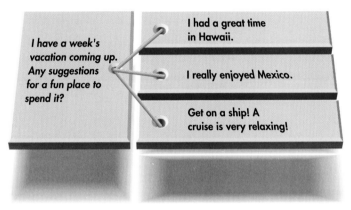

I have a week's vacation coming up. Any suggestions for a fun place to spend it?

I had a great time in Hawaii.

I really enjoyed Mexico.

Get on a ship! A cruise is very relaxing!

Thread

A thread is an article and all replies to the article. A thread may include an initial question and the responses from other readers.

SORTING ARTICLES

When displaying a list of articles in a newsgroup, you can usually view several pieces of information about the articles. This information includes the name of the person who wrote the article, the subject of the article and the date the article was sent to the newsgroup.

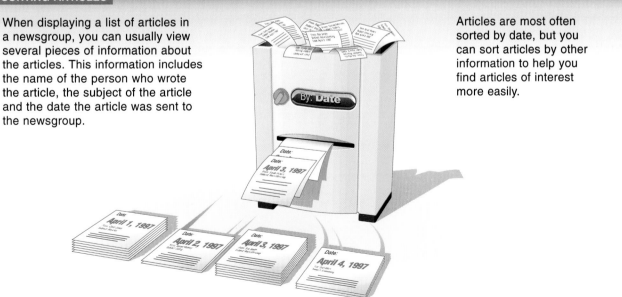

By: Date

Date:
April 3, 1997

Date:
April 1, 1997

Date:
April 2, 1997

Date:
April 3, 1997

Date:
April 4, 1997

Articles are most often sorted by date, but you can sort articles by other information to help you find articles of interest more easily.

NEWSREADERS

A newsreader is a program that lets you read and post articles to newsgroups.

Web Browsers

Many Web browsers have a newsreader built-in. This means the look and feel of the newsreader is very similar to the look and feel of the Web browser. If you are familiar with using the Web browser, you should find the built-in newsreader easy to learn and use. Newsreaders built into Web browsers often do not have as many features as separate newsreader programs.

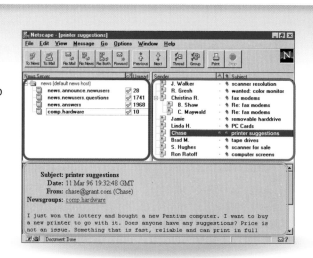

■ This area displays a list of newsgroups.

■ This area displays a list of all the articles in the selected newsgroup.

■ This area displays the contents of a single article.

NEWSREADER PROGRAMS

Free Agent

Free Agent is one of the most popular newsreaders available. It has many features such as the ability to ignore articles with a specific subject.

There is no charge for Free Agent, but you can purchase an upgraded version of the program that offers even more features.

Free Agent is available at the following Web site:

http://www.forteinc.com/forte

Gravity

Gravity is a newer newsreader for computers using Windows 95 or Windows NT. Gravity uses a system called "rules" to allow you to perform many tasks automatically. For example, you can use rules to tell the newsreader to display only articles containing specific words.

Gravity is available at the following Web site:

http://www.microplanet.com/products.stm

InterNews

InterNews is a newsreader for Macintosh computers. InterNews allows you to screen, or hide, specific newsgroups. This feature is useful for blocking access to any offensive newsgroups.

InterNews is available at the following Web site:

http://www.dartmouth.edu/~moonrise

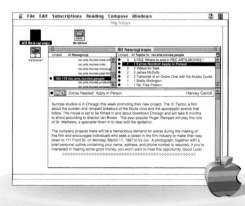

NEWSREADERS

E-Mail

Many Usenet newsreaders come with an e-mail program built-in. Posting and retrieving articles with a newsreader is very similar to sending and receiving messages with an e-mail program.

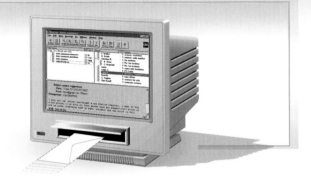

Read and Write Offline

Some people have to pay for the time they spend accessing the Internet. This includes the time spent reading and writing newsgroup articles. Many newsreaders save you money by allowing you to read and write newsgroup articles when you are not connected to the Internet.

Spell Checking

Before posting an article for thousands of people to read, you should check the article for spelling errors. Many newsreaders automatically spell check articles for you. If your newsreader does not have a built-in spell checker, you can write your article in a word processor that has a spell checker and then post the article.

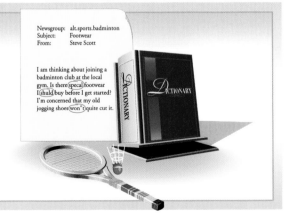

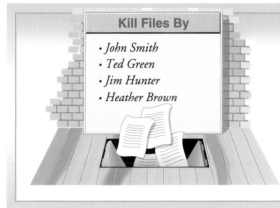

Kill Files

Most newsreaders allow you to enter the name of a person into a file called a kill file. This tells the newsreader to automatically delete any articles posted by that person. Kill files are useful when someone is frequently posting inappropriate articles to a newsgroup.

Filters

Some newsgroups can receive over a thousand articles in one day. Some newsreaders provide filters that allow you to display only the type of articles you want to read. This lets you find the information you need without having to read every article in the newsgroup.

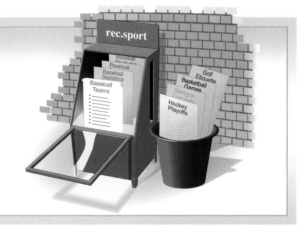

Privacy

There are many companies that index all articles posted to Usenet newsgroups. This allows people on the Internet to search the indexed articles and monitor which newsgroups you post to and how often you post articles.

To keep your articles private, some newsreaders now let you automatically mark an article so it will not be indexed by search companies.

SUBSCRIBE TO NEWSGROUPS

You subscribe to a newsgroup you want to read on a regular basis.

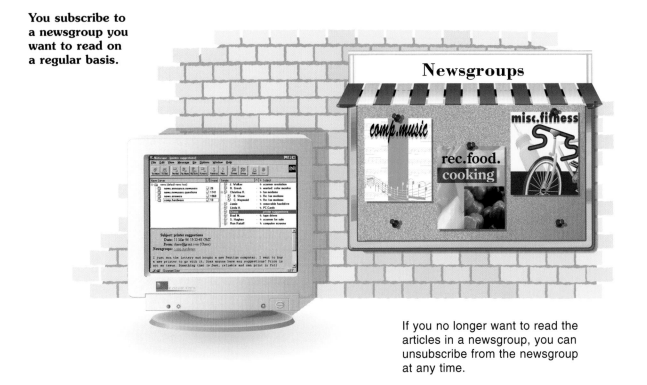

If you no longer want to read the articles in a newsgroup, you can unsubscribe from the newsgroup at any time.

Moderated Newsgroups

Some newsgroups are moderated. In these newsgroups, a volunteer reads each article and decides if the article is appropriate for the newsgroup. If the article is appropriate, the volunteer posts the article for everyone to read.

Moderated newsgroups may have the word "moderated" at the end of the newsgroup name (example: **sci.military.moderated**).

In an unmoderated newsgroup, all articles are automatically posted for everyone to read.

New Newsgroups

New newsgroups are created every day. A newsreader lets you display a list of all the newsgroups that have been created since the last time you checked.

Once you have the names of new newsgroups, you can subscribe to the newsgroups.

Similar Newsgroups

There is often more than one newsgroup that discusses a particular topic. For example, the topics discussed in the **alt.books.reviews** newsgroup are similar to the topics discussed in **rec.arts.books**.

If you are interested in a specific topic, you should subscribe to all the newsgroups that discuss the topic.

Removed Newsgroups

When a newsgroup becomes very popular, it is often removed and split into several smaller, more specific groups. For example, a newsgroup for buying and selling items might be split into two smaller newsgroups: one for computer-related items and the other for non-computer-related items.

If a newsgroup you are subscribed to is removed, you may be able to subscribe to the new, smaller newsgroups.

WORK WITH ARTICLES

READ AN ARTICLE

You can read articles to learn the opinions and ideas of thousands of people around the world.

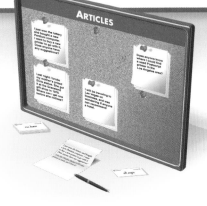

New articles are sent to newsgroups every day. You can browse through articles of interest just as you would browse through the morning newspaper.

PRINT AN ARTICLE

You can produce a paper copy of an article you find interesting.

POST AN ARTICLE

You can post, or send, a new article to a newsgroup to ask a question or express an opinion. Thousands of people around the world may read an article you post.

If you want to practice posting an article, send an article to the **alt.test** newsgroup. You will receive automated replies to let you know you posted correctly. Do not send practice articles to other newsgroups.

REPLY TO AN ARTICLE

You can reply to an article to answer a question, express an opinion or supply additional information. A reply you post to a newsgroup is called a followup.

Reply to an article only when you have something important to say. A reply such as "Me too" or "I agree" is not very informative.

Original Article

The baked potatoes that I serve to my guests are not very appetizing. How can I make them more appealing?

Reply

How can I make them more appealing?

Try adding sour cream and paprika, and then sprinkle chili powder on top. Bon appetit!

Quoting

When you reply to an article, make sure you include part of the original article. This is called quoting. Quoting helps readers identify which article you are replying to. To save readers time, make sure you delete all parts of the original article that do not directly relate to your reply.

Private Replies

You can send a reply to the author of an article, the entire newsgroup or both.

If your reply would not be of interest to others in a newsgroup or if you want to send a private response, send a message to the author instead of posting your reply to the entire newsgroup.

PICTURES AND PROGRAMS IN ARTICLES

In addition to plain text, you can get pictures and programs from newsgroup articles.

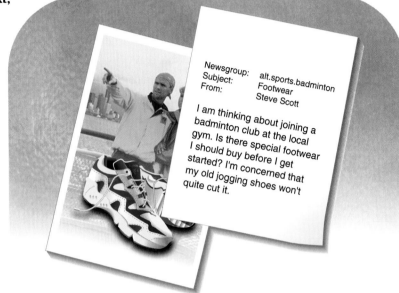

Newsgroup: alt.sports.badminton
Subject: Footwear
From: Steve Scott

I am thinking about joining a badminton club at the local gym. Is there special footwear I should buy before I get started? I'm concerned that my old jogging shoes won't quite cut it.

Binaries

Pictures and programs you get from a newsgroup are called binary files, or binaries. Binaries are posted to newsgroups in articles.

Note: Many pictures posted to newsgroups may contain adult-oriented or offensive material.

Newsgroups

There are many newsgroups available for people who want to exchange binary files. Before you send pictures or programs to a newsgroup, check the FAQ for the newsgroup to see if there are any restrictions on binaries.

Most binary newsgroups are restricted to a specific type of file. Binary newsgroups have the word "binaries" in the name, such as **alt.binaries.clip-art**

Newsreaders

Many newsreaders are available for accessing binaries people have posted to Usenet newsgroups. Because binaries can take a long time to transfer, most newsreaders allow you to select which binaries you want to get before transferring the binaries to your computer.

Post a Picture or Program

When you post a picture or program in a newsgroup article, your newsreader automatically changes the picture or program into a binary file.

ARTICLE 1

```
Z`...n^~9h*...n"o@
U n^9h.[...n^...g`>
,.'.D~..an^,9h..vy
Hn^..n^ H..K g.--n.
..]n^9h.*..?>>dJ1
..bf.Jdg...,...D
```

ARTICLE 2

```
`p./.N=\RY..Hn^..
n^ H..an^,9h...n^~9
hHn^..n^9h..vy?>>d
J1 n^9h.[./.N=\RY.
D~..an^,9h..vyHn^.
.n^ H..K
```

Binary files are often very large. If the binary is too large to fit in one article, the newsreader will split the binary into smaller sections and post each section as a separate article.

Get a Picture or Program

Before you can use a picture or program from an article, you must decode the binary to change it into the original picture or program. Many newsreaders can decode binary files automatically.

If your newsreader does not have this ability, you can use a program called a decoder. If a binary is posted as several articles, you can select one of the articles to decode the entire binary file.

NEWS SERVERS

A news server is a computer that stores newsgroup articles. News servers are run and maintained by Internet access providers.

When you send an article to a newsgroup, the news server you are connected to keeps a copy of the article and then distributes the article to other news servers around the world.

The amount of articles sent to newsgroups each day is approximately equal to the amount of information in a set of encyclopedias.

After a few days or weeks, articles are removed from a news server to make room for new articles. When you see an article you want to keep, make sure you print or save the article.

Administrators

Each news server has an administrator who decides which newsgroups will be available on the server. The administrator may also restrict each user's access to certain newsgroups.

For example, you may not be able to access certain newsgroups if you are under 18.

News Feeds

News servers on the Internet exchange new newsgroup articles frequently to ensure that all the servers always have all the available articles.

The articles that are sent from one news server to another are referred to as a news feed. A news server may get news feeds from several different servers.

Open News Servers

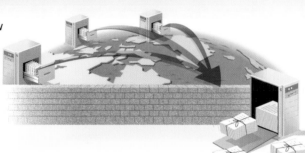

If you want to access a newsgroup that is not available on your news server, you can use an open news server. Open news servers often offer newsgroups that discuss topics for specific geographic regions.

You can get a list of open news servers at the following Web site:

http://www.geocities.com/Hollywood/2513/news.html

NEWSGROUP ETIQUETTE

Newsgroup etiquette refers to the proper way to behave when sending messages to a newsgroup.

Writing Style

Thousands of people around the world may read an article you post to a newsgroup. Before posting an article, make sure you carefully reread the article.

ARTICLE

I just won the lottery, I bought a new Pentium computer. I want to buy a new printer to go with it. Does anyone has any suggestions? Price is probably not an issue but it might be. I would prefer something that are fast, reliable and can print in full color. Thanks in advance.

○ -Grammar errors
? -Misleading

Make sure your article is clear, concise and contains no spelling or grammar errors.

Also make sure your article will not be misinterpreted. For example, not all readers will realize a statement is meant to be sarcastic.

Subject

The subject of an article is the first item people read. Make sure your subject clearly identifies the contents of your article. For example, the subject "Read this now" or "For your information" is not very informative.

Expensive Fishing Equipment

I really enjoy fishing, but all of my equipment is relatively inexpensive. My fishing budget keep telling me to upgrade to costly reels and lures. Will actually make a different is good technique more than spending lots of ...

B.J. Wils...

Hot Springs in Arkansas

My wife and I are planning to take a trip through Arkansas next year. We've heard there are some lovely hot springs the state, but we don't know where. Could someone give us some advice?

Thanks, Mark C...

Mountain Bike Tune-ups

This is my first year of mountain biking, and so far I've been doing my own tune-ups. But lately my bike hasn't performed well. For example, the chain slips when I switch gears. I'm wondering if I should pay a mechanic to do my tune-ups. Is it worth it?

Thanks, Ronald Hill

Read Articles

Read the articles in a newsgroup for a week before posting an article. This is called lurking. Lurking is a good way to learn how people in a newsgroup communicate and prevents you from posting information others have already read.

Read the FAQ

The FAQ (Frequently Asked Questions) is a document containing a list of questions and answers that often appear in a newsgroup.

The FAQ is designed to prevent new readers from asking questions that have already been answered. Make sure you read the FAQ before posting any articles to a newsgroup.

Post to the Appropriate Newsgroup

Make sure you post an article to the appropriate newsgroup. This ensures that people interested in your questions and comments will see your article.

Do not post an article to several inappropriate newsgroups. This is called spamming. Spamming is particularly annoying when the article serves a commercial purpose, such as selling a product or service.

CHILDREN AND NEWSGROUPS

There are many newsgroups available for children. These newsgroups cover topics such as television shows, books and pen pals. You should closely monitor any newsgroups your children subscribe to.

alt.kids-talk

alt.tv.simpsons

rec.toys.misc

misc.kids

Adult Supervision

Constant adult supervision is the best way to ensure that children do not access inappropriate information in newsgroups. You should read all the articles in a newsgroup for a week before you let your children access the newsgroup.

Select Newsgroups

If your newsreader allows you to read and compose messages offline, you can control which newsgroups your children access and which articles they respond to. You can get messages from only the newsgroups you feel are appropriate for your children. After the children have read the messages and written replies, you can read the replies before reconnecting to the Internet and posting the replies.

Personal Information

Children should never include personal information about themselves in an article they post to a newsgroup.

Personal information includes their address, which school they go to and the location of any clubs or organizations they participate in.

Post Anonymously

Many newsreaders let you use a nickname and fake e-mail address when posting articles to a newsgroup.

If children want to participate in a newsgroup that is not specifically for children, they should use a phony name and e-mail address so they do not reveal their true identity.

E-Mail Responses

When you post an article to a newsgroup, you often receive e-mail messages from people commenting on the article.

Ignore any information in an e-mail reply that does not directly relate to the information in the article you posted. If you receive an inappropriate e-mail message, do not respond to the message.

FIND ARTICLES WITH DEJA NEWS

Deja News is a database containing articles people have posted to Usenet newsgroups.

Deja News is located at:
http://www.dejanews.com

Available Articles

The Deja News database currently stores over 80 million articles dating back to March 1995. Deja News hopes to eventually make all articles that have been posted since 1979 available for searching.

Keep Articles Private

Deja News automatically places any article that is posted to a Usenet newsgroup in the Deja News database. When an article appears in the database, anyone on the Internet can find and read the article. If you do not want your article included in the Deja News database, type **x-no-archive: yes** as the first line of the article.

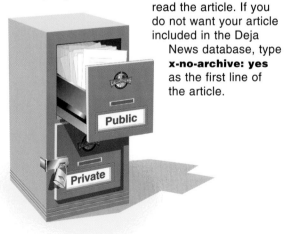

TYPES OF DEJA NEWS SEARCHES

Quick Search

Quick Search is the fastest and easiest way to search for an article. When you enter a word, Deja News searches its database and displays a list of all articles containing the word you specified.

You can read articles displayed in the list and send an e-mail message to the author of an article. Quick Search only searches for articles posted in the last several weeks.

Power Search

Power Search provides many options you can use to narrow your search. You can search for several words at one time. You can also specify whether you want to search recent articles or older ones.

Author Profile

You can use Deja News to find information on anyone who posts an article to a Usenet newsgroup.

If you know the e-mail address of a person, you can find out how many articles they have posted and which newsgroups they have posted to. You can even read the articles if you wish.

Newsgroups are divided into separate sections, or categories. The newsgroups in each category discuss the same general topic. Newsgroup categories are also referred to as the Newsgroup Hierarchy.

Local Newsgroups

Many Internet service providers create newsgroups that are only accessible to customers of the ISP. The service provider usually uses these newsgroups to offer technical support to customers. These local newsgroups often start with the name of the ISP.

Create a Newsgroup

You can create your own newsgroup in the **alt** category. You can find information about creating your own newsgroup in the **news.admin.hierarchies** and **news.admin.misc** newsgroups. Your service provider may also be able to help you create your own newsgroup.

alt (alternative)

General interest discussions that can include unusual or bizarre topics. Some of the material available in the **alt** newsgroups may be offensive to some people.

Examples

alt.binaries.sounds.movies

alt.college.fraternities

alt.fan.actors

alt.music.alternative

alt.ufo.reports

biz (business)

Business discussions that are usually more commercial in nature than those in other newsgroups. Advertising is allowed in many **biz** newsgroups and lists of job openings are available.

Examples

biz.books

biz.books.technical

biz.jobs.offered

biz.marketplace.computers.discussion

biz.marketplace.services

MAIN NEWSGROUP CATEGORIES

comp (computers)

Discussions of computer hardware, software and computer science. The **comp** newsgroups are a good source of technical support for computer-related problems.

Examples

comp.graphics

comp.lang.pascal.borland

comp.laser-printers

comp.security.misc

comp.sys.laptops

k12 (kindergarten to grade 12)

Discussions of topics concerning kindergarten to grade 12 students. Most of the people who contribute to the **k12** newsgroups are teachers or educators.

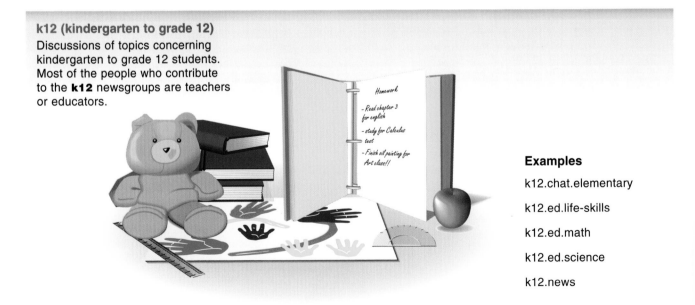

Examples

k12.chat.elementary

k12.ed.life-skills

k12.ed.math

k12.ed.science

k12.news

misc (miscellaneous)

Discussions of various topics that may overlap topics discussed in other categories. Many of the topics discussed in the **misc** newsgroups can also be found in the **alt** newsgroups.

Examples

misc.consumers.house

misc.education

misc.entrepreneurs

misc.forsale

misc.taxes

news

Discussions about newsgroups in general. Topics range from information about the newsgroup network to advice on how to use it. The **news** newsgroups also contain a large amount of information concerning the technical details of Usenet.

Examples

news.admin.misc

news.announce.newgroups

news.announce.newusers

news.answers

news.newusers.questions

rec (recreation)

Discussions of recreational activities and hobbies. The messages in the **rec** newsgroups are often more entertaining than informative.

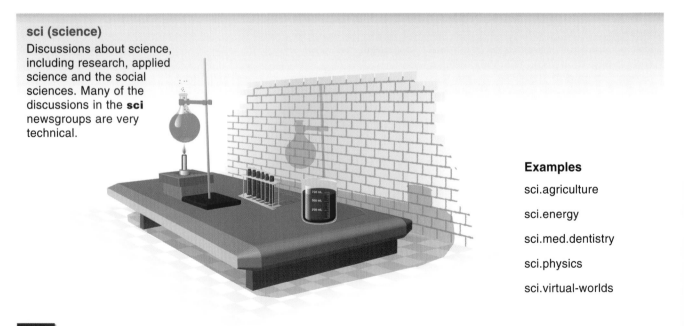

Examples

rec.arts.movies.reviews

rec.autos

rec.food.recipes

rec.games.board

rec.sport.football.pro

sci (science)

Discussions about science, including research, applied science and the social sciences. Many of the discussions in the **sci** newsgroups are very technical.

Examples

sci.agriculture

sci.energy

sci.med.dentistry

sci.physics

sci.virtual-worlds

soc (social)

Discussions of social issues, including world cultures and political topics. The **soc** newsgroups also contain information about selected regions around the world.

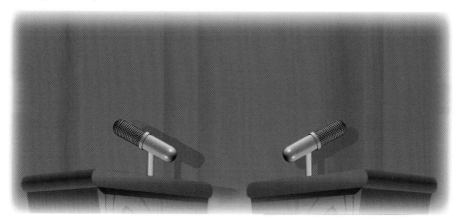

Examples

soc.college

soc.culture.caribbean

soc.history

soc.politics

soc.women

talk

Debates and long discussions, often about controversial subjects. Most of the messages in the **talk** newsgroups are quite long and very well-researched.

Examples

talk.bizarre.funny

talk.environment

talk.philosophy.misc

talk.politics

talk.rumors

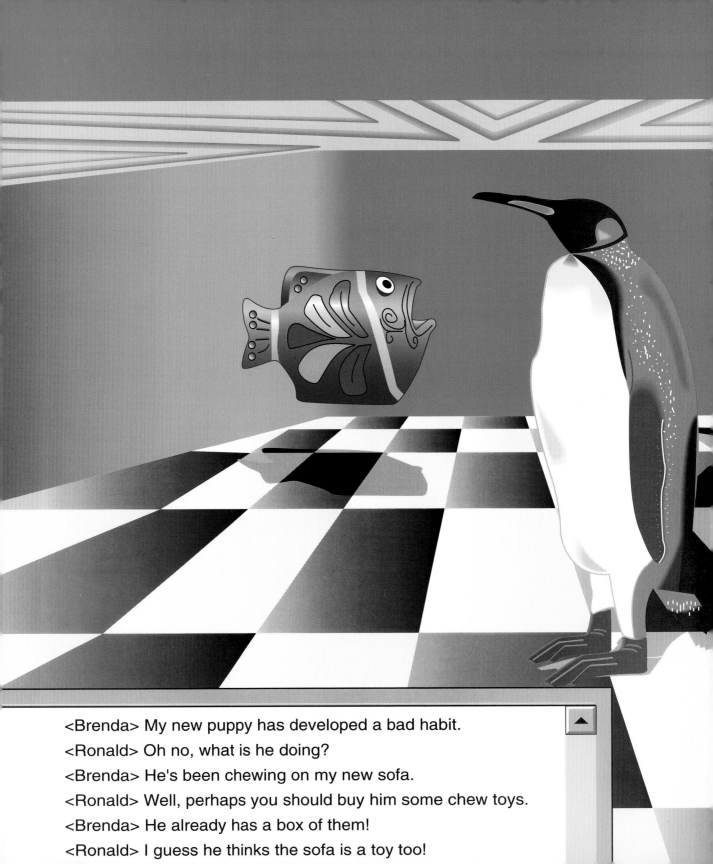

<Brenda> My new puppy has developed a bad habit.

<Ronald> Oh no, what is he doing?

<Brenda> He's been chewing on my new sofa.

<Ronald> Well, perhaps you should buy him some chew toys.

<Brenda> He already has a box of them!

<Ronald> I guess he thinks the sofa is a toy too!

Chat

Why is chatting one of the most popular features of the Internet? This chapter introduces you to Web-based chat, voice chat, video chat and much more.

INTRODUCTION TO CHAT

You can instantly communicate with people around the world by typing back and forth. This is called chatting. Chatting is one of the most frequently used features of the Internet.

TYPES OF CHAT

Text-Based

Text-based chat is the oldest and most popular type of chat on the Internet. You can have conversations with one or more people. When you type text, the text appears on the screen of each person participating in the conversation. Since text transfers quickly across the Internet, you do not need a high-speed connection to the Internet.

> Tanya - I need some help! I have to write an essay about an unusual animal. Any ideas?
>
> Chris - How about the dodo bird?
>
> Robin - My teacher assigned me the same project and I couldn't find any info on the dodo bird.
>
> Chris - What animal did you write about?
>
> Robin - I wrote about the sea cucumber. It's unusual and there's lots of info out there.

Multimedia

Multimedia chat is one of the newer features of the Internet. You can now have voice conversations and communicate with other people through live video over the Internet. Since sound and video transfer slowly across the Internet, you should have a high-speed connection to use multimedia chat.

Education

Many students use chat to discuss assignments and get help from fellow students and instructors. This is particularly useful for people who are too far away from schools or colleges to attend classes on a regular basis.

Entertainment

Most people use chat as a form of entertainment. You can use chat to meet new friends from all over the world.

Keep in Touch

Chatting is a low-cost way to stay in touch with friends or relatives who have access to the Internet. Many people use Internet chat to communicate with friends and family members in other parts of the world.

Product Support

Some product manufacturers are now using Internet chat to provide technical support for their customers. Technical support people make themselves available for chatting so customers can ask questions and get answers instantly.

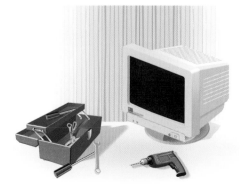

INTERNET RELAY CHAT

Internet Relay Chat (IRC) is a system that allows you to chat with other people on the Internet. To use IRC, you must connect to a computer called an IRC server. Each IRC server is connected to a network of other IRC servers around the world.

Name and E-Mail Address
Before connecting to IRC, you must enter your name and e-mail address. Most IRC servers will not let you connect unless you enter a valid e-mail address. You can enter a fake name if you wish to remain anonymous, but other people may still be able to find out your real name.

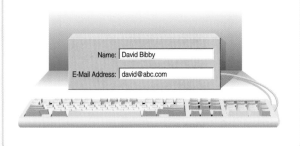

Nicknames
You must choose a nickname for yourself before using IRC. If another person is already using your nickname, you must choose a different nickname. A nickname can have up to nine letters. You can often register your nickname so no one else can use the nickname.

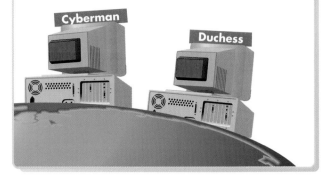

Channels

There are many channels, or chat groups, you can join on IRC. Each channel usually focuses on a specific topic. A channel name often tells you the theme of the discussion.

A # symbol in front of a channel name means the channel is available to people all over the world.

An & symbol in front of a channel name means the channel is available only to people using the IRC server you are connected to.

Channel Operators

If you try to join a channel that does not exist, IRC will create a new channel and make you the channel operator. When you leave the channel, you are no longer the channel operator.

A channel operator controls who may join the channel. Channel operator nicknames display the @ symbol. Some channels are permanently controlled by programs called "bots," which is short for robots.

IRC NETWORKS

An IRC network is a group of IRC servers located all over the world that are connected together to allow people to chat. There are many IRC networks you can connect to.

Undernet

Undernet is a smaller version of EFNet. Undernet users tend to be more friendly than EFNet users.

http://www.undernet.org

EFNet

EFNet is the largest of all the IRC networks and has the most unruly users.

http://www.efnet.org

NewNet

Unlike other IRC networks, NewNet allows users to vote on issues that involve changes to the network.

http://www.newnet.net

DALnet

DALnet is an IRC network where you can permanently register your own nickname and leave messages for other people.

http://www.dal.net

Different IRC networks are not connected to each other. This means that if you want to chat with people on an EFNet IRC channel, you must connect to the EFNet network.

IRC PROGRAMS

You need an IRC program to be able to connect to a server on an IRC network.

Most IRC programs are very easy to use and provide many features you can customize to suit your needs. For example, some IRC programs allow you to change the font and color of the text that appears on your screen to make the text easier to read.

There are many IRC programs available on the World Wide Web. You can try these programs free of charge for a limited time:

Ircle (Macintosh)
http://www.xs4all.nl/~ircle

mIRC (Windows)
http://www.mirc.co.uk

PIRCH (Windows)
http://www.bcpl.lib.md.us/
~frappa/pirch.html

You can use commands when chatting on IRC to control activities such as joining an IRC channel or sending private messages to other people.

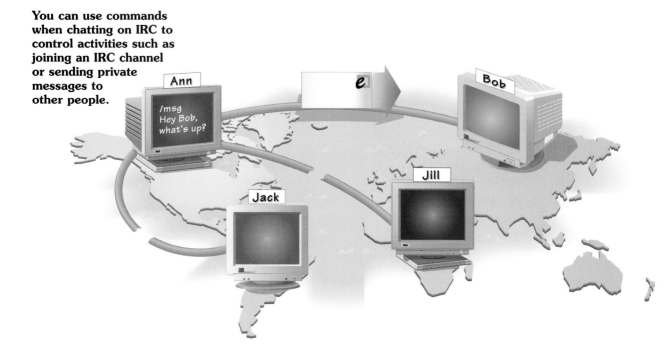

Enter Commands

When chatting on IRC, you usually enter text into an area at the bottom of your screen to communicate with other people in the channel. You can also use this area to enter IRC commands. Each command you type must start with a slash (/). Other people in the channel cannot view commands you enter.

IRC Programs

You can use IRC commands with any IRC program, although some programs do not support all the latest commands. Some programs also have extra commands that only work with that IRC program. Many IRC programs allow you to execute commands by selecting buttons.

IRC COMMANDS

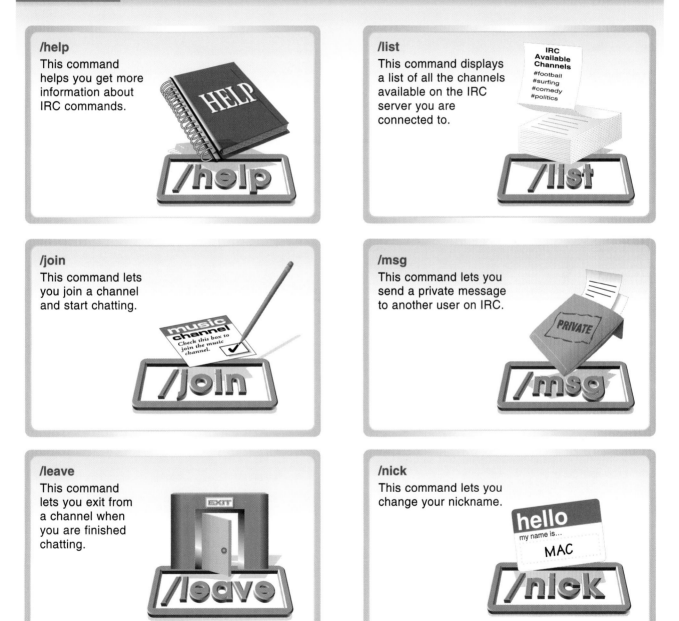

/help

This command helps you get more information about IRC commands.

/list

This command displays a list of all the channels available on the IRC server you are connected to.

IRC Available Channels
#football
#surfing
#comedy
#politics

/join

This command lets you join a channel and start chatting.

music channel
Check this box to join the music channel.

/msg

This command lets you send a private message to another user on IRC.

PRIVATE

/leave

This command lets you exit from a channel when you are finished chatting.

EXIT

/nick

This command lets you change your nickname.

hello
my name is...
MAC

Just like at a cocktail party, there is a proper way to behave when chatting with people on IRC. Ignoring IRC etiquette could get you disconnected or permanently banned from the IRC server.

Respect Language

People from many different countries use IRC. This means many channels might be used by people who do not speak the same language as you. When you join a channel, respect the language being used in the channel. If you want to discuss the topic in your own language, start a new channel for people who speak the same language as you.

Automatic Greetings

Many software programs allow you to automatically say hello to anyone new who joins the channel you are in. These automatic greetings are not appreciated by users of IRC. Only greet people if you know them or wish to start chatting with them.

Complaining to IRC Administrators

Each IRC channel has a channel operator who can ban people from the channel for any reason. If you have been banned from a channel, do not complain to the system administrator of the IRC server. These IRC administrators are responsible for maintaining the servers and do not have time to settle disputes between IRC users.

Flooding

Sending a lot of text to a channel at once is called flooding. Many IRC programs have built-in controls to restrict the amount of information you can send at once.

If you flood a channel, you may be disconnected or permanently banned from the IRC server.

Cloning

You can easily start several IRC programs on your computer and connect to IRC using different nicknames. This is known as "cloning." Since cloning is often used to cause mischief, many IRC servers can now find out if you are connected using a different nickname.

Cloning may cause you to be banned from using the IRC server in the future.

WEB-BASED CHAT

Web-based chat is one of the newer features of the Internet. Web-based chat is fun and very easy to use.

Web Browser

All the chat networks on the World Wide Web require only that you have a Web browser to participate. Some chat Web sites use newer features such as Java.

If you have trouble participating in a Web-based chat site, make sure you have the latest version of your Web browser.

Cost

Most of the chat services on the Web are free. Many of the Web-based chat sites receive income from companies that advertise on the Web sites.

This means the chat sites do not have to charge users. Some chat services allow you to participate for free for a limited time, but then you must pay a fee to continue chatting.

WebChat Broadcasting System

WebChat claims to be the largest Web-based chat network on the Internet. WebChat often offers chat rooms hosted by experts such as personal finance counselors and travel consultants.

You can access WebChat at the following Web site:

http://www.wbs.net

Ichat

Ichat is very similar to Internet Relay Chat. When you enter text, anyone in the same chat room, or group, will see the text you entered. Ichat is much easier to set up and use than Internet Relay Chat.

You can access Ichat at the following Web site:

http://www.ichat.com

Worlds Chat

Worlds Chat allows you to walk around and talk to other people in a three-dimensional world. People are represented by objects, such as penguins and chess pieces, known as avatars.

You must have the Worlds Chat software before you can chat in Worlds Chat. You can get the Worlds Chat software at the following Web site:

http://www.worlds.net

VOICE CHAT

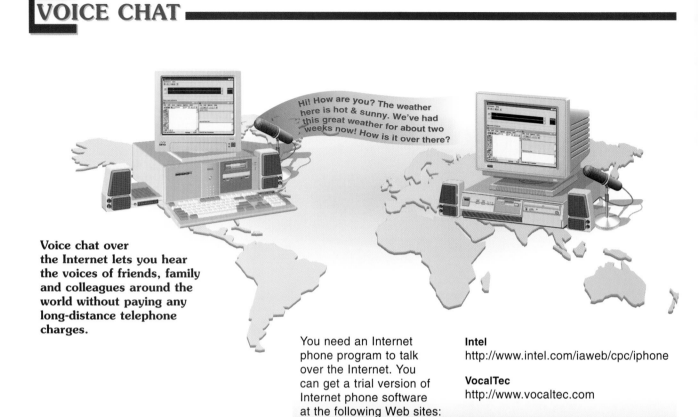

Hi! How are you? The weather here is hot & sunny. We've had this great weather for about two weeks now! How is it over there?

Voice chat over the Internet lets you hear the voices of friends, family and colleagues around the world without paying any long-distance telephone charges.

You need an Internet phone program to talk over the Internet. You can get a trial version of Internet phone software at the following Web sites:

Intel
http://www.intel.com/iaweb/cpc/iphone

VocalTec
http://www.vocaltec.com

Equipment

You need specific equipment to talk over the Internet. Your computer must have a sound card with speakers and a microphone attached. A half-duplex sound card lets only one person talk at a time. A full-duplex sound card lets two people talk at once, just as you would talk on the telephone. Full-duplex sound cards are the best type of sound card for voice chat.

Contact Other People

If you want to communicate with another person using voice chat, you must both use the same type of Internet phone software. You can usually find a directory of people who use your Internet phone program at the Web site where you got the program. You can browse through the directory to find people you want to chat with.

Video chat lets you see the person you are talking to, even if the other person is on the other side of the world. You can also talk to several people at once.

You need a special program to communicate using video chat on the Internet. You can get a trial version of video chat software at the following Web sites:

CU-SeeMe
http://goliath.wpine.com/cu-seeme.html

V-Fone
http://www.summersoft.com

To communicate with other people using video chat, you must all use the same type of video chat software.

Equipment

Before you can use video chat, you must have a video camera for your computer. You can buy an inexpensive video camera that attaches to the top of your monitor. You can also use a regular video camera if you have a special expansion card for your computer.

Image Quality

If you are using a modem to transfer video images, the quality of the images may be poor. Some video chat programs can help increase the quality of video images. Make sure you try out a video chat program before purchasing to see the quality of the images.

POPULAR IRC CHANNELS

#beginner
Help for Internet beginners.

#chatzone
General discussions and chit-chat.

#café
A relaxing place to hang out.

#geek
Where computer addicts can be found.

#cars
Discussions about all types of cars.

#history
General and specific discussions about history.

#cats
All things to do with cats.

#international
Where people from different nations gather.

#ircnewbies
Ask questions about
IRC chat.

#nhl
National Hockey
League.

#mlb
Major League
Baseball.

#pcgames
Talk about games for
home computers.

#nba
National Basketball
Association.

#politics
Chat about politics
around the world.

#new2irc
This should be your
first stop on IRC.

#windows
Discussions about the
Microsoft Windows
operating systems.

Telnet

Why is telnet a useful resource for exploring information on the Internet? Find out in this chapter.

INTRODUCTION TO TELNET

Telnet lets you use
your computer to
run programs and
access information
on another computer
on the Internet.

Text-Based

When you use telnet to connect to another
computer, you see lines of text with no images.
You type simple text commands to communicate
with the computer. You can often also select
options from a list. Information can sometimes
take a moment to appear on your screen.

Bulletin Board Services

Many Bulletin Board Services (BBSs) are
available on the Internet. You can telnet
to some BBSs to access huge amounts
of information not available anywhere
else. Unlike the Internet, BBSs tend to
be well-organized and make it easy to
find files and read information.

Information Services

Telnet is the easiest way to access information stored in databases on computers in large organizations.

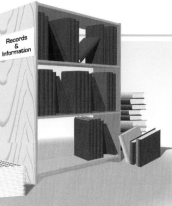

Many government agencies and universities make the information stored on their computers available by using telnet.

Account Management

Some Internet service providers require you to use telnet to access their computers.

Once you are connected to a computer at the service provider, you can change your password or the way your account is set up. These systems are usually easy to use and often provide step-by-step menus to help you.

Technical Support

Most Internet service providers let customers access the technical support department by e-mail.

If you are having problems setting up or running your e-mail program, you can use telnet to connect to the Internet service provider and request technical support.

TELNET PROGRAMS

You must use a telnet program to connect to another computer on the Internet. There are many telnet programs available.

Logging

When using telnet to access information on another computer, you may not be able to fit all the information on the screen at one time. Many telnet programs let you log, or save, the information in a file on your own computer. Logging allows you to review the information later.

File Transfer

Many of the new telnet programs allow you to transfer files from one computer to another. Using a telnet program to transfer files is convenient because you no longer need a separate program to transfer files to or from a computer you are connected to.

TELNET PROGRAMS

Microsoft Telnet

Windows 95 comes with a built-in telnet program called Microsoft Telnet. Microsoft Telnet is usually installed automatically when the Windows 95 operating system is installed.

Microsoft Telnet lets you customize several options, such as changing the font and color of the text displayed on your screen.

NetTerm for Windows

NetTerm is a sophisticated telnet program. Apart from standard telnet access over the Internet, NetTerm also has a wide range of features, such as an easy-to-use directory of popular telnet sites.

NetTerm is available at the following Web site:

http://starbase.neosoft.com/~zkrr01

NCSA Telnet for the Macintosh

NCSA Telnet is one of the oldest and most reliable telnet applications available for computers that use the Macintosh operating system. NCSA Telnet has many options that let you set up the program to suit your needs.

NCSA Telnet is available on the World Wide Web at:

ftp://ftp.ncsa.uiuc.edu/Mac/Telnet

CONNECT USING TELNET

A telnet service is any computer that allows you to access information by telnet. Most telnet services are easy to use. Some services may require you to enter information before you can use the service.

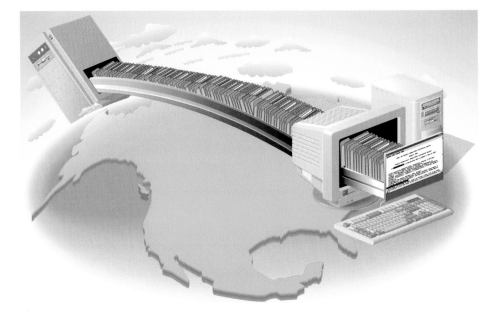

Login Name

Most telnet services require that you enter a login name and password to access information. Telnet services on the Internet often tell you which login name to use before you connect to the computer. Many telnet services allow you to log into the computer using the login name "guest" with no password.

Terminal Type

Terminal type describes the language a telnet program uses to communicate with the computer you are connecting to. Most computers require you to specify the terminal type you use. Each terminal type uses specific keyboard keys to perform specific tasks. VT100 is the most common terminal type and works with most computers.

Host Address

The host address of a telnet service is the name or number of the computer that makes the information available. Most telnet programs allow you to enter the name of the computer you want to connect to, such as "main.maran.com"

Some telnet programs require you to enter the number of the computer you want to connect to, called the IP number. A host address number consists of four numbers separated by periods (.), such as 207.156.23.1

Port Number

A telnet port number refers to a specific location on a computer where information is available. The port number for most telnet services is 23.

If the host address ends with a colon (:) followed by a number (example: main.maran.com:33), the number after the colon is the port number. If there is more than one telnet service on the same computer, each telnet service will have a different port number.

A shell account provides an easy-to-use interface that lets you read or change information stored on another computer.

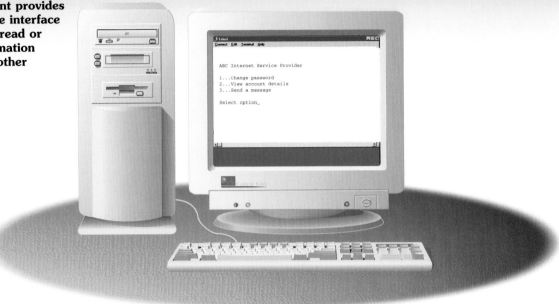

```
ABC Internet Service Provider

1...Change password
2...View account details
3...Send a message

Select option_
```

Internet Service Providers

You can use telnet to connect to a computer at your Internet service provider to change account information such as your password or home address. Some ISPs do not allow people to use telnet to connect to the computers.

If you need to use telnet to connect to your service provider, you should ask the ISP if it is possible to set up a shell account.

Unix

Many Internet service providers use the Unix operating system on their computers. If you have a shell account on a Unix computer, you may see the $ symbol when you connect to the computer. This means you can enter commands to display information.

COMMON UNIX COMMANDS

There are many commands you
can use to perform tasks when
using a shell account.

password

The Password command
lets you change your
password.

cp

The Copy command
lets you make copies
of files or directories.

cd

The Change Directory
command lets you
move to a different
directory.

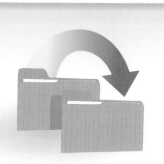

rm

The Remove command
lets you delete files or
directories.

mkdir

The Make Directory
command lets you
create a new directory.

ls

The List command lets
you display the contents
of the directory you are
in.

INTERESTING TELNET SITES

CARL Corporation
This site contains many databases providing information for and about libraries all over the world. You must use the login name "pac" to access this site.

pac.carl.org

FedWorld
This telnet site for the United States government contains a wide range of information.

fedworld.gov

CDnow!
You can use this telnet site to shop for CDs, cassettes and video tapes.

cdnow.com

Geographic Name Server
This site allows you to find information about a city by typing in the city name or a zip code.

martini.eecs.umich.edu
(Port = 3000)

CHAT
This site allows you to search databases of various information using plain English commands.

debra.doc.ca (Port = 3000)

Greenwich Mean Time
This site tells you the time according to a federal atomic clock.

india.colorado.edu (Port = 13)

Cleveland FreeNet
You can explore and use this freenet system for free for a limited time.

freenet-in-a.cwru.edu

Libraries of Stanford University
You can use this site to search for information in the libraries of Stanford University. You must use the login name "socrates" to access this site.

forsythetn.stanford.edu

Library of Congress Information System

At this telnet site, you can search the records of the Library of Congress.

locis.loc.gov

University of Maryland

This site stores the CIA Factbook, which provides information about most of the countries in the world.

info.umd.edu

Pennsylvania State University

This site contains consumer-related news and bulletins. You must use the login name "WORLD" to access this site.

psupen.psu.edu

U.S. Food and Drug Administration

At this telnet site, you can find a database of health information. You must use the login name "bbs" to access this site.

fdabbs.fda.gov

Rutgers University - INFO

This site contains lots of material you can search through, including dictionaries, a thesaurus and the Bible.

info.rutgers.edu

Weather Underground

You can find skiing reports as well as weather forecasts for most major cities in the world.

madlab.sprl.umich.edu (Port = 3000)

Subway Navigator

This site will tell you how long it will take to get from one station to another on most of the subway systems in the world.

metro.jussieu.fr (Port = 10000)

WildStar

This site lets you try out IRC to chat with other people on the Internet.

telnet.wildstar.net (Port = 6677)

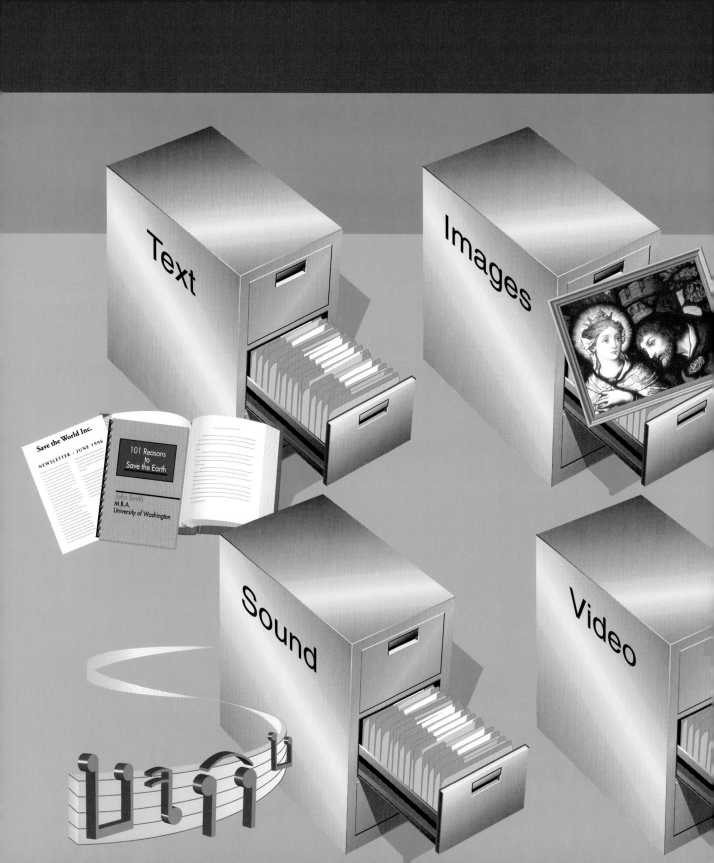

FTP

What is FTP and why is it useful? In this chapter you will learn how FTP allows you to search for information on computers around the world.

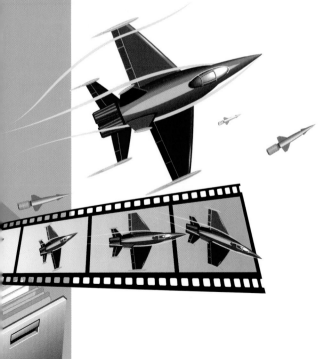

INTRODUCTION TO FTP

File Transfer Protocol (FTP) lets you look through files stored on computers around the world and copy files that interest you.

FTP SITE

An FTP site is a computer on the Internet that stores files. FTP sites are maintained by colleges, universities, government agencies, companies and individuals. There are thousands of FTP sites scattered across the Internet.

Private FTP Sites

Some FTP sites are private and require you to enter a password before you can access any files. Many corporations maintain private FTP sites to make files available to their employees and clients around the world.

Anonymous FTP Sites

Many FTP sites are anonymous. Anonymous FTP sites let you access files without entering a password. These sites store huge collections of files that anyone can download, or copy, free of charge.

Files at FTP sites are stored in different directories.

Directories

Just as folders organize documents in a filing cabinet, directories organize information at an FTP site.

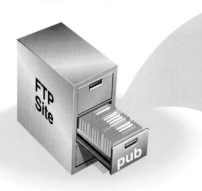

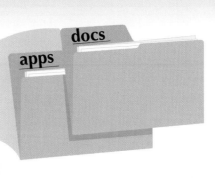

Most FTP sites have a main directory called **pub**, which is short for public. The pub directory contains subdirectories and files. Most subdirectory names indicate what type of files the subdirectory contains. Common subdirectory names include **apps** for application programs and **docs** for text files and documents.

File Names

Every file stored at an FTP site has a name and an extension, separated by a period (.). The name describes the contents of a file. The extension usually identifies the type of file.

manual.txt

Development in the Western sense is to i economy. It Third Worl production especially order to c the World of develop requires n machiner fuels for c countries

porsche.gif

readme

index

Most well-established FTP sites include files that describe the rest of the files offered at the site. Look for files named "readme" or "index"

TYPES OF FILES

Text

You can get interesting documents for research and for enjoyment. You can obtain books, journals, electronic magazines, computer manuals, government documents, news summaries and academic papers.

Look for these extensions:

.asc .doc .htm .html .msg .txt .wpd

Images

You can get images, such as computer-generated art, museum paintings and pictures of famous people.

Look for these extensions:

.bmp .eps .gif .jpg .pict .png

Sound

You can get theme songs, sound effects, clips of famous speeches and lines from television shows and movies.

Look for these extensions:

.au .ra .ram .snd .wav

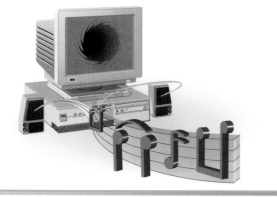

Video

You can get movie clips, cartoons, educational videos and computer-generated animation.

Look for these extensions:

.avi .mov .mpg

Programs

You can get programs to use on your computer, such as word processors, spreadsheets, databases, games and much more.

Look for these extensions:

.bat .com .exe

Public Domain

Public domain programs are free and have no copyright restrictions. You can change and distribute public domain programs as you wish.

Free !

Freeware

Freeware programs are free but have copyright restrictions. The author may require you to follow certain rules if you want to change or distribute freeware programs.

Free!
(with restrictions)

◆ You must include the author's name (and this file) wherever the program is distributed.

◆ You must not sell this program.

◆ You must n___ ___ ___ this program in

◆ You must ___ registrati___

Freeware Program

Shareware

You can try a shareware program free of charge for a limited time. If you like the program and want to continue using it, you must pay the author of the program.

Try Before You Buy

COMPRESSED FILES

Many large files stored at FTP sites are compressed, or squeezed, to make them smaller.

Compressed Files

A smaller, compressed file requires less storage space and travels more quickly across the Internet.

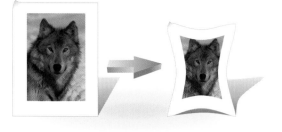

Archived Files

A program usually consists of a large group of files. Programs are often compressed and then archived, or packaged, into a single file. This prevents you from having to transfer each file individually to your computer.

Decompressed Files

Before you can use a compressed or archived file on your computer, you usually have to expand or unpack the file using a decompression program.

You can often get a decompression program for free at sites where you copy files. Popular decompression programs include PKZip for IBM-compatible computers and StuffIt for Macintosh computers.

FILE EXTENSIONS

Compressed or archived files have an extension that describes the type of compression program used.

ZIP

You can use a file that has the .zip extension with most computer systems. You can get a program that will decompress .zip files at the following Web site:

http://www.winzip.com

ARJ

You can use a file that has the .arj extension with computers running DOS or Windows operating systems. Although .arj files are not as common as .zip files, they are still regularly found on the Internet.

TAR

The .tar extension indicates a file that has been archived. TAR is often used with Unix operating systems. You can use most decompression programs to unarchive a .tar file.

HQX

You can use a file that has the .hqx extension with Macintosh computers. You can get a program for decompressing .hqx files at the following Web site:

http://www.aladdinsys.com

Other common file extensions include:

.bin   .gz   .gzip   .seq   .tgz   .z

Before you can get a file from an FTP site, you will need an FTP program. There are many programs available.

Operating Systems

Most operating systems, such as Windows 95 and Unix, already have a basic FTP program built-in. These FTP programs are text-based. This means that you enter words to perform tasks and you can view information only as text on your computer screen.

Web Browsers

You can use your Web browser to get files from an FTP site. You cannot use your Web browser to transfer files to an FTP site. To access an FTP site using your Web browser, type **ftp://** followed by the name of the FTP site.

WS_FTP

WS_FTP is one of the most popular FTP programs for Windows. You can use WS_FTP to access FTP sites and to organize files in your own directories on your Internet access provider's computer.

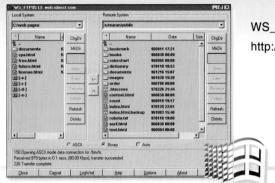

WS_FTP is available at:

http://www.ipswitch.com

Fetch

Fetch is the most popular FTP program for the Macintosh operating system. Fetch is useful if you perform a lot of repetitive tasks at FTP sites. You can record the actions you perform. You can then replay the actions instead of performing them again step-by-step.

Fetch is available at:

http://www.dartmouth.edu/pages/softdev/fetch.html

CuteFTP

CuteFTP is an FTP program for Windows. The left side of the CuteFTP screen displays a list of the files on the FTP site. The right side of the screen displays the files on your computer. You select the files you want to transfer and then drag the files to the new location.

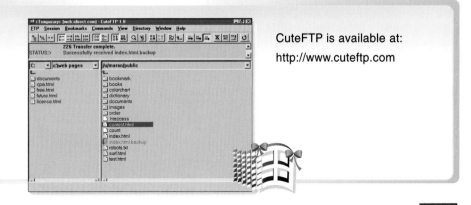

CuteFTP is available at:

http://www.cuteftp.com

CONNECT TO AN FTP SITE

Before connecting to an FTP site, you may have to enter some information into your FTP program.

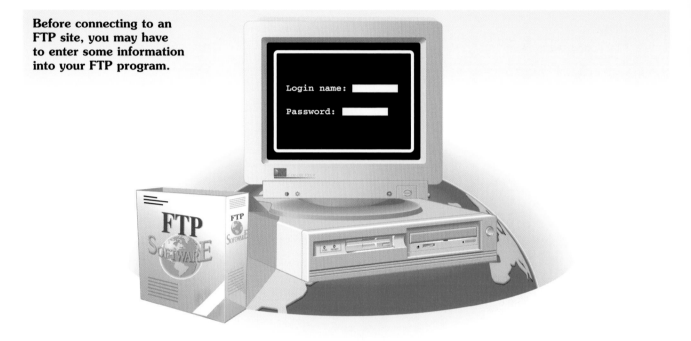

Host Address

The host address of an FTP site is the name or number of the computer that stores the FTP site.

A host address name usually starts with "ftp", such as "ftp.maran.com". A host address number, or IP number, consists of four numbers separated by periods (.), such as 207.156.23.1

User Identification

Before you can access an FTP site, you must enter a login name and password. Most FTP sites let you use the name "anonymous" as your login name.

The password is usually your e-mail address. Some FTP sites require you to type a hyphen before your e-mail address. Do not enter the password you use to connect to your Internet access provider.

Port Number

An FTP port number refers to a specific location on a computer where FTP information is stored. The port number for most FTP sites is 21.

If the host address ends with a colon (:) followed by another number (example: 207.156.23.1:47), the number after the colon is the port number. Most FTP programs automatically set the port number for you.

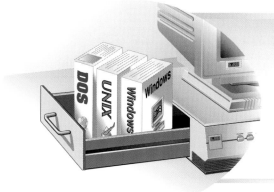

Host Type

The host type refers to the type of operating system running on the computer where the FTP files are stored. Most FTP programs can automatically detect what type of operating system is being used.

Transfer Type

ASCII and binary are two ways to transfer files to and from an FTP site. Use a binary transfer for information such as programs, compressed files or sound files.

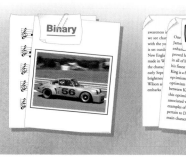

Use an ASCII transfer for text files. Most FTP programs can automatically choose the correct type of transfer for you.

Avoid Traffic Jams

Each FTP site can only let a certain number of people use the site at once. If you get an error message when you try to connect, the site may already have as many people connected as it can handle.

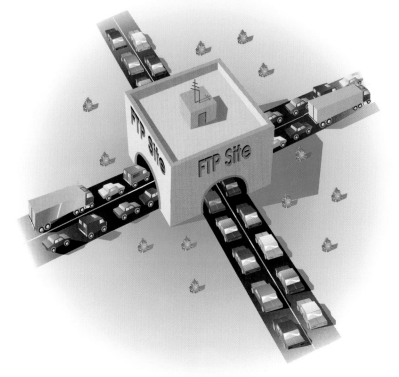

Connect at a Different Time

Try accessing FTP sites outside business hours, such as at night and on the weekend. Fewer people use the Internet at these times.

Use Mirror Sites

Some popular FTP sites have mirror sites. A mirror site stores exactly the same information as the original site but is usually less busy. A mirror site may also be geographically closer to your computer, which can provide a faster and more reliable connection.

Mirror sites are updated on a regular basis to ensure that the files available at the original site are also available at the mirror site.

Compatibility

Just because you can transfer a file to your computer does not mean you can use the file. Make sure you only get files that can work with your type of computer. Many FTP sites have separate directories for Macintosh and IBM-compatible computers.

Hardware and Software

You may need special hardware or software to use files you get from an FTP site. For example, you need a sound card and speakers to hear sound files.

Viruses

Files stored at FTP sites may contain viruses. A virus is a destructive computer program that can disrupt the normal operation of a computer.

You should frequently make backup copies of the files on your computer and always check for viruses before you use any file copied from an FTP site.

Anti-virus programs are available at most major FTP sites.

Archie is a search
tool used to locate
files stored on FTP
sites on the Internet.

Archie Servers

An Archie server is a computer that stores a list
of all the files available from FTP sites on the
Internet. All Archie servers on the Internet contain
the same list of files. To use Archie to find files,
you must connect to an Archie server.

File Names

Using Archie to find files is only efficient if you
know part of the name of the file you are looking
for. Archie servers contain thousands of file names
and very brief descriptions of files. Since many
people do not use descriptive names for their files,
it can be difficult to find what you are looking for.

1423.txt
2afile.doc
prog2.exe
452ex.gif
46bnl.com
draw.bat
pac.jpg

Archie Programs

You can get a program to connect to and search an Archie server. When you start the program and specify the name of the file you are looking for, the program displays a list of FTP sites containing the file. You can get an Archie program at the following Web site:

http://dspace.dial.pipex.com/town/square/ cc83/wsarchie.htm

Telnet

You can use a telnet program to quickly connect to an Archie server. You can use the name "archie" as a login name. You do not need a password. To search for a file, type **PROG** followed by the name of the file you want to find. You can use telnet to connect to an Archie server at:

archie.internic.net

World Wide Web

The World Wide Web is the easiest way to connect to an Archie server. When you specify the name of the file you are looking for, the Web page displays a list of all the FTP sites containing the file. You can find an Archie Web site at:

http://www.lerc.nasa.gov/archieplex/ doc/form.html

FIND FILES WITH SHAREWARE.COM

Shareware.com is a newer way to get files from the Internet. Shareware.com has access to hundreds of thousands of files.

You can find Shareware.com at the following Web site:

http://www.shareware.com

Virtual Software Library

Shareware.com has a Virtual Software Library (VSL), which is a directory of files stored on computers all over the Internet, including FTP sites. When you search for a file, Shareware.com displays a list of computers that store the file.

Files

A shareware program is a program you can use for a limited time before paying for the program. Many of the files available at Shareware.com are shareware programs. Shareware.com also makes demonstration editions of programs as well as program upgrades available free of charge.

Search Types

You can perform three different types of searches with Shareware.com.

Quick Search

When you type a word describing the file you want to find and specify the type of operating system you are using, Shareware.com displays a list of 25 results.

Simple Search

A Simple Search is similar to a Quick Search but you can enter two words to describe the file. You can also choose to display more than 25 results.

Power Search

Power Search provides many options to help you search for a file. You can use several words to describe the file you want to find.

Transfer Files

After you search for a file, Shareware.com displays every computer on the Internet that stores the file.

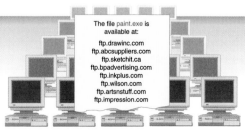

The file paint.exe is available at:

ftp.drawinc.com
ftp.abcsuppliers.com
ftp.sketchit.ca
ftp.bpadvertising.com
ftp.inkplus.com
ftp.wilson.com
ftp.artsnstuff.com
ftp.impression.com

You can access one of these computers to transfer the file to your computer.

POPULAR FTP SITES

Anonymous FTP Server
At this site you can find listings of other FTP sites available on the Internet.

iraun1.ira.uka.de

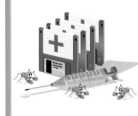

Mcafee Software
This FTP site contains shareware programs that protect your computer against viruses.

ftp.mcafee.com

Conjelco
This FTP site contains many files for fans of casino gaming and card games.

ftp.conjelco.com

mirror.apple.com
You can find an extensive collection of software and information for Macintosh computers at this site.

mirror.apple.com

The INESC Archive
This site hosts electronic text versions of the complete works of William Shakespeare.

porthos.inescn.pt/pub/doc/ Fiction/Shakespeare

OAK Software Repository
One of the most popular FTP sites on the Internet, this site contains all types of programs for many types of computers.

oak.oakland.edu

LEO - Link Everything Online
This site stores all types of information about music and related topics, including a collection of song lyrics.

ftp.leo.org/pub

ServiceTech
You can find a collection of all sorts of software programs and text files at this FTP site.

ftp.servtech.com

TSX-11

This Massachusetts Institute of Technology FTP site contains a wide range of information and software.

tsx-11.mit.edu

Walnut Creek CD-ROM

This site provides a collection of software and information that is also available at computer stores on CD-ROM discs.

ftp.cdrom.com

University of Nevada

This site contains a lot of useful information for photographers.

ftp.nevada.edu/pub/photo

Windows FTP Archive

A collection of shareware and freeware programs for computers that use a Windows operating system.

ftp.winsite.com

Usenet FAQ Directory

This FTP site provides a collection of all the available FAQs for Usenet newsgroups.

rtfm.mit.edu/pub/usenet-by-group

The World

One of the oldest sites available on the Internet, The World site contains a wide variety of documents.

ftp.std.com

Vaasa University, Finland

A huge collection of programs and information files for all types of computers can be found at this site.

garbo.uwasa.fi

Ziff-Davis

This FTP site contains files from popular computing magazines such as PC Week and PC Magazine.

ftp.zdnet.com

Gopher

How can Gopher be used to find interesting and useful information on the Internet? Learn how in this chapter.

Gopher is a tool that lets you use text and menus to browse through information on the Internet.

Gopher Menu

The Jimi Hendrix Experience
The history of the Beatles
Woodstock facts
Suggested music for flower ch...

Gopher Sites

A Gopher site is a computer that stores files you can view or transfer to your computer. Gopher sites are often referred to as Gopher holes and are usually found at universities, colleges, government agencies or companies. Gopher sites usually have the word "gopher" in the name of the site.

The First Gopher Site

The first Gopher site appeared at the University of Minnesota where Gopher was developed. The Golden Gopher is the mascot of the university. The University of Minnesota Gopher site displays the locations of most Gopher sites on the Internet.

You can access the University of Minnesota Gopher site through the World Wide Web at:

gopher.tc.umn.edu

UNIVERSITY OF **M** MINNESOTA

Gopherspace

Gopherspace is the name given to all the information stored at Gopher sites around the world. Gopherspace is similar to the World Wide Web.

When you select a link describing a document at a Gopher site, the document that appears on your screen may be stored at a Gopher site on the other side of the world.

Gopher Menus

When you first access a Gopher site, you will see a main menu offering a list of categories. When you select a category from the menu, a new menu appears displaying a list of subcategories.

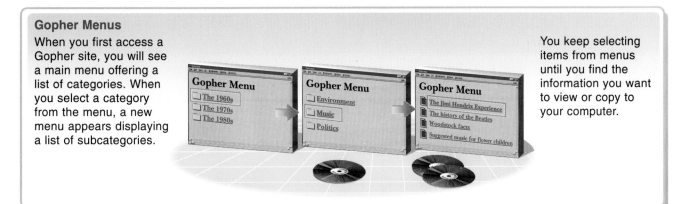

You keep selecting items from menus until you find the information you want to view or copy to your computer.

The Future of Gopherspace

Many Gopher sites are being replaced by Web sites. Since the World Wide Web is easier to use and organize than Gopherspace, many companies and organizations now place information on a Web site instead of a Gopher site.

Gopher sites are still a very important resource for academic information, but they will eventually become extinct.

Using a Gopher program is the fastest way to display information stored at Gopher sites. There are many Gopher programs available.

Bookmarks

Just as you can use bookmarks to mark your favorite pages in a book, you can use the bookmark feature in most Gopher programs to mark your favorite Gopher sites on the Internet. The bookmark feature lets you store the addresses of Gopher sites you frequently visit so you do not have to remember and constantly retype the addresses.

Helper Applications

Many Gopher programs do not have the ability to display images or play sound files. If you want to use any of these features, you need to use a helper application. Helper applications help a Gopher program display or play files the program cannot display or play on its own.

WSGopher

WSGopher is the most popular Gopher program for computers using the Microsoft Windows operating system. WSGopher offers many features, such as allowing you to select which Gopher site you want to appear on your screen each time you start the program.

WSGopher is available on the World Wide Web at:

http://sageftp.inel.gov/dap/gopher.htm

TurboGopher

TurboGopher is a Gopher program for Macintosh computers. You can use TurboGopher to retrieve files from FTP sites on the Internet.

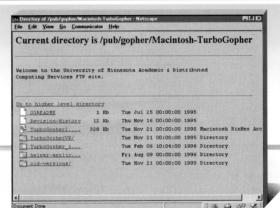

TurboGopher is available on the World Wide Web at:

ftp://boombox.micro.umn.edu/pub/gopher/Macintosh-TurboGopher

Web Browsers

You can also use your Web browser to access Gopher sites. Web browsers are ideal for people who occasionally access Gopher sites. Web browsers provide an easy way to view information on Gopher sites, but browsers usually do not offer as many features as Gopher programs.

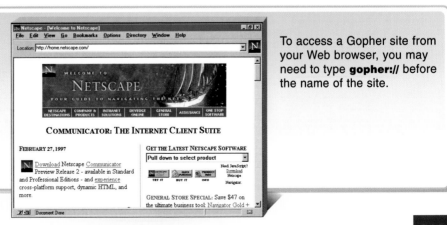

To access a Gopher site from your Web browser, you may need to type **gopher://** before the name of the site.

CONNECT TO A GOPHER SITE

Before connecting to a Gopher site, you may have to enter some information into your Gopher program. Some Gopher programs now enter the information automatically.

Name: Internet Wiretap
Address: wiretap.spies.com
Port #: 70

Host Address

The host address of a Gopher site is the name or number of the computer that stores the Gopher site. A host address name usually starts with "gopher", such as "gopher.tamu.edu". A host address number, or IP number, consists of four numbers separated by periods (.), such as 207.155.23.1

Port Number

A Gopher port number refers to a specific location on a computer where Gopher information is available. The port number for most Gopher sites is 70. If the host address ends with a colon (:) followed by another number (example: 207.155.23.1:82), the number after the colon is the port number.

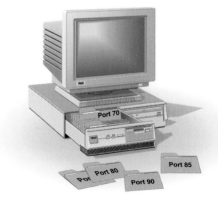

Most Gopher sites offer search programs that help you find information you are looking for.

Veronica

Veronica is a program that lets you search all of Gopherspace for information. The program regularly collects information from Gopher sites around the world. When you enter a word or phrase, Veronica displays a menu of Gopher sites containing the word or phrase you specified.

Jughead

Jughead is a search tool that allows you to specify which area of a Gopher site you want to search. Jughead is a useful search tool for finding specific information in a large Gopher site. For example, if you need to find specific information about a company, such as sales figures, you can use Jughead to search only the area of the company's Gopher site that stores that information.

You do not need to search all of Gopherspace to find the information you want.

POPULAR GOPHER SITES

There are many Gopher sites on the Internet where you can find interesting and useful information.

Australian National Botanic Gardens

This extensive site offers a wide variety of botanical information as well as many other useful resources.

osprey.erin.gov.au

Consumer Product Safety Commission

This U.S. government agency makes many safety reports and publications available at its Gopher site.

cpsc.gov

Children's Literature

You can read the full text of many classic books for children at this site.

gopher.cascade.net/11/ pub/Literature/Childrens

Cycling Phone Numbers

This Gopher site provides a list of telephone numbers for companies that make bikes or cycling accessories.

draco.acs.uci.edu:1071/ 00/tech.supp.phone

Internet Wiretap

This huge site provides all types of government information and books.

wiretap.spies.com

University of Minnesota

The oldest Gopher site on the Internet, this site stores lots of interesting and useful information.

gopher.tc.umn.edu

Library Catalogs

You can search for information in libraries around the world at this site.

libgopher.yale.edu

USCgopher

The Gopher site at the University of Southern California offers links to many other Gopher sites around the world.

cwis.usc.edu

National Institute of Health

You can find lots of information about various aspects of health care at this site.

gopher.nih.gov

Weather Machine

Find weather statistics and pictures from around the world at this site.

wx.atmos.uiuc.edu

University of Illinois

This Gopher site is a good starting point for people who want to explore Gopherspace.

gopher.uiuc.edu

The World

This site provides various information, including a list of non-profit organizations you can access using Gopher.

gopher.std.com

Multi-Player Games

What types of multi-player games are available? In this chapter you will learn about traditional multi-player games, multi-user dungeons, network games and much more.

A multi-player game is a game that lets you use a computer to play against one or more opponents. Multi-player games are becoming one of the most popular uses of the Internet.

Types

There are many types of multi-player games on the Internet. One of the simplest types is Play By E-Mail (PBEM) games, where players simply e-mail their moves to other players. Arcade-style games are also very popular. You can play fast-paced action or adventure games against players on the other side of the world.

Flexible

There are hundreds of multi-player games you can play over the Internet. Everyone can find a game that suits their interests. You can find games that require several hours a day or just a few minutes each week. You can choose from simple card games to complex games requiring science and math skills.

Interactive

Playing multi-player games on the Internet allows you to interact and communicate with people from all over the world. Some games even have their own associations where players can meet each other face to face.

Challenging

Even though you can play most games against a computer, many games are better when you play them against other people. Most computers react the same way each time you play a game. When you play a game against a person, the game will be different every time.

Competitive

Playing games on the Internet can be very competitive. Almost every game played on the Internet has a site on the World Wide Web that displays a list of winners.

Some games even have tournaments for the top players of the game.

PLAY BY E-MAIL GAMES

Play By E-Mail (PBEM) games are a convenient and simple way to participate in multi-player games. To play an e-mail game, you need an e-mail account set up on your computer.

Move 10:

White bishop C2 to B3

Types of Games

There are several types of e-mail games. To play the simplest type, such as chess or checkers, you exchange moves with your opponent by e-mail. In more complex types of games, all the players e-mail their moves to one computer. The computer processes all the moves and controls the flow of the game.

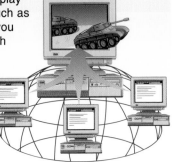

Benefits

E-mail games allow each player to play at a convenient time, so you do not have to constantly be at your computer to play. You can also easily find an opponent whose skill level matches your skill level. Playing people with similar skill levels usually makes games more fun.

Global Diplomacy

Global Diplomacy is a strategy game where you attempt to conquer the world. Each player controls a region of the world. You must negotiate and make pacts with other players to win the game.

You can find out more about Global Diplomacy at the following Web site:

http://www.islandnet.com/ ~dgreenin/emg-game.htm#GD

Food Chain

This mathematics-based game allows you to design your own species of animal or plant and then release it into the jungle. Depending on how well you designed the species, it will either evolve or become extinct.

You can find out more about Food Chain at the following Web site:

http://www.pbm.com/~lindahl/ pbm_list/descriptions/ food_chain.html

Electronic Knock Out

In this game, you are the manager of a group of boxers. You control the characteristics of each boxer in your group. Each week you submit your boxers for fights against boxers controlled by other players.

You can find out more about Electronic Knock Out at the following Web site:

http://www.vivi.com

TRADITIONAL MULTI-PLAYER GAMES

Some of the first games to be played on the Internet were traditional board and card games, such as backgammon and bridge.

Players

Most traditional multi-player games are board or card games. When you play these types of games on the Internet, you can quickly find opponents and start a game. You can play these games with friends and family members, even if they are located on the other side of the world.

How about a game of cards?

Board Games

Many people find it difficult to play board games when the board is displayed on a computer monitor. To avoid this problem, you can set up the game board in front of your computer. You can then move the game pieces on the board according to what appears on your computer screen.

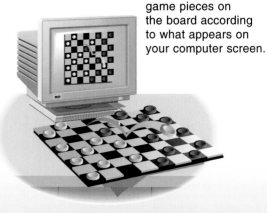

Backgammon

There are many places on the Internet where you can play backgammon. The WWW Backgammon Page has information about backgammon and provides links to help you play with other people on the Internet. The WWW Backgammon Page is located at:

http://www.gamesdomain.com/backgammon

Bridge

Bridge is one of the most popular card games in the world. You can use the Internet to learn and practice the game. When you are ready to play against a real person, you can easily find an opponent on the Internet. You can find more information about bridge on the Internet at:

http://www.bridgeplayer.com

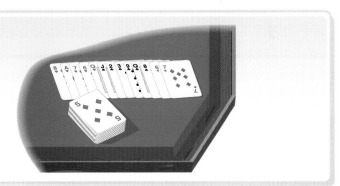

Chess

Chess is one of the oldest games in the world. When you play chess on the Internet, you can easily find an opponent whose skill level matches your skill level. The Internet Chess Club hosts over 15,000 chess matches each day. The Internet Chess Club is located at:

http://www.hydra.com/icc

MULTI-USER DUNGEONS

Multi-User Dungeons (MUDs) are one of the oldest and most popular forms of multi-player games on the Internet.

MUDs allow you to interact with other people in a variety of different worlds.

Virtual Worlds

MUDs take place in virtual worlds. When you play a MUD, you assume the identity of a character living in the virtual world. You type commands to make your character perform actions like running or talking. You also type commands to make changes to the world, such as creating or destroying buildings.

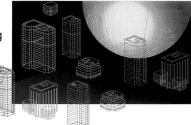

MUSHs, MOOs and MUCKs

MUSHs, MOOs and MUCKs are types of MUDs. The name of each type refers to the type of software that runs the MUD. MUSHs, MOOs and MUCKs each use their own commands to perform tasks in the virtual world. Each type of MUD also has its own set of rules. Some types let you fight with other characters, while other types do not.

London by Gaslight

This game is set in London, England at the turn of the century, during the time of Jack the Ripper, Sherlock Holmes and Dr. Jekyll and Mr. Hyde.

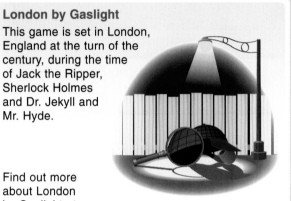

Find out more about London by Gaslight at:

http://www.ultranet.com/~rogerc/lbg_intro.html

Masquerade

This game is for fans of vampires, werewolves and things that go bump in the night.

Find out more about Masquerade at:

http://www.iquest.net/bc/masq

VenusMUSH

This game is set in the year 2041, when all the inhabitants of Earth have relocated to the planet Venus and are governed by an alien race.

Find out more about VenusMUSH at:

http://mama.indstate.edu/users/bones/venus/Venus.html

AuroraMUSH

AuroraMUSH is a pleasant place to visit with a very social theme. Players are encouraged to interact with other characters.

Find out more about AuroraMUSH at:

http://galaxy.neca.com/~soruk

COMMERCIAL SOFTWARE GAMES

Often when you buy a commercial software game, you can only play the game against the computer. Many games now let you play against other people on the Internet.

Get Software

You can buy commercial software games at many computer stores. There are also many commercial software games available on the Internet.

If you are playing a commercial software game with other people, each person must have their own copy of the game.

Connecting

Connecting to other people on the Internet to play a commercial software game is often very simple. Commercial software games are usually played on one computer on the Internet. To play the game, you simply connect to this computer.

Quake

Quake is one of the most popular commercial software games. In this three-dimensional game, you walk around computer-generated worlds looking for your enemies. Up to 16 people can participate in a game.

You can find more information about Quake at the following location:

http://www.idsoftware.com

Command & Conquer

Command & Conquer is a military strategy game you can play with up to three other people at a time.

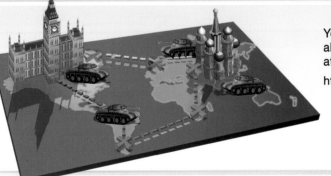

You can find more information about Command & Conquer at the following Web site:

http://www.westwood.com

Big Red Racing

Big Red Racing lets you race against up to five different people at a time. You can choose strange vehicles to race in, such as a snow plow or a boat.

You can find more information about Big Red Racing at:

http://www.worldserver.pipex.com/bigred/racing/index.html

NETWORK GAMES

Many games are designed to be played on a network. You can often also play these games with other people on the Internet.

Networks

Unlike many games that let you play only against your computer, games are now designed to let several people compete against each other on a network. A network is a group of computers connected together to share information and equipment. The equipment needed to set up a network is relatively inexpensive, so many players and their friends set up small networks at home.

Kali

Kali is a program that lets you play network games against other people on the Internet. When you use Kali to play a network game on the Internet, Kali makes the game think you are playing on a network. You can find out more about Kali at the following Web site:

http://www.kali.net

POPULAR NETWORK GAMES

MechWarrior 2

In MechWarrior 2, you control a fully armed and mobile robot and try to knock out your opponents before they get you. MechWarrior 2 is a very popular game and can be played by up to four people.

You can find MechWarrior 2 on the Web at:

http://www.activision.com

Diablo

Diablo is a Dungeons and Dragons type role-playing game. Your quest is to find the fiend Diablo, who is responsible for destroying your village.

You can get more information about Diablo at the following Web site:

http://www.blizzard.com/diablo/diablo.htm

Duke Nukem 3D

In Duke Nukem 3D, you see the world through the eyes of your character in the game. You fight against monsters or against other people playing on the Internet.

You can get Duke Nukem 3D on the Web at:

http://www.3drealms.com

Intranets

What are intranets? This chapter introduces you to networks and intranets. You will also learn about intranet Web sites, software, applications and security.

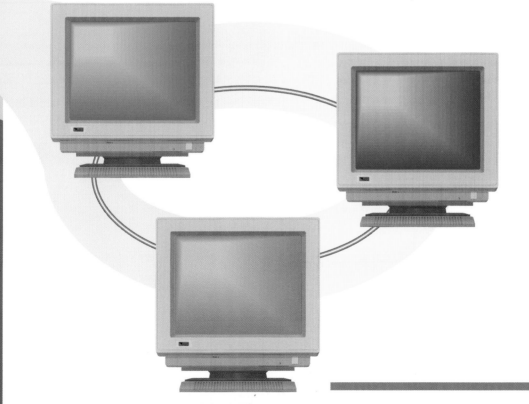

INTRODUCTION TO NETWORKS

A network is a group of connected computers that allow people to share information and equipment.

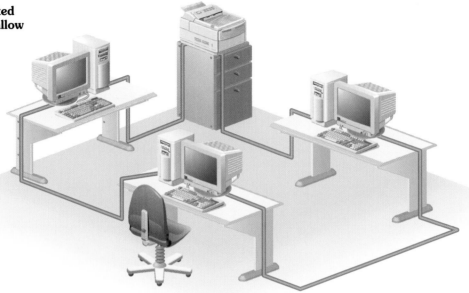

Local Area Network

A Local Area Network (LAN) is a network that connects computers within a small geographic area, such as a building.

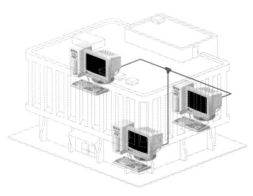

Network Operating Systems

Network Operating Systems (NOS) are designed for powerful computers, called network servers, to ensure that all parts of a network work together smoothly and efficiently. Network operating systems allow network servers to store programs and information so other computers on the network can access the programs and information.

NETWORK ADVANTAGES

Work Away From Office

When traveling or at home, you can connect to the network at work to exchange messages and files.

Share Information

Networks let you easily share information and programs. You can exchange documents, electronic mail, video, sound and images.

Eliminate Sneakernet

Sneakernet refers to physically carrying information from one computer to another to exchange information. A computer network eliminates the need for sneakernet.

Share Equipment

Computers connected to a network can share equipment, such as a printer or modem.

NETWORK ADMINISTRATOR

A network administrator manages the network and makes sure the network runs smoothly. A network administrator may also be called a network manager, information systems manager or system administrator.

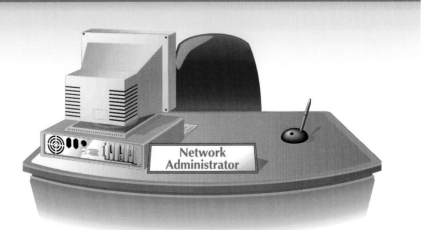

Network Administrator

An intranet is a network, similar to the Internet, within a company or organization. Intranets offer many of the features and services that are available on the Internet.

Files

Document sharing is one of the main reasons a company or organization would set up an intranet. You can place documents you would not display on the Internet, such as workplace procedures or a company newsletter, on an intranet. Employees can also use an intranet to update or install new software programs. Transferring software from an intranet is much easier than using floppy disks or CD-ROM discs.

Multimedia

Information transfers much faster over an intranet than over the Internet. This makes it easy to transfer sound and video files that would take too long to transfer over the Internet. You can use an intranet to easily distribute product demonstrations and training videos to anyone connected to the intranet.

E-Mail

Many companies use e-mail systems that only allow employees to exchange simple text. Intranets allow companies to use the same type of e-mail system that is found on the Internet.

This lets employees send much more information in an e-mail message, such as a spreadsheet or a word processing document.

Newsgroups

Many organizations use newsgroups that are similar to the Usenet newsgroups found on the Internet. Employees can use newsgroups to share information about the company or about a specific project.

People can post questions or updates to the newsgroups so their colleagues can view the information.

Chat

Companies can set up chat channels, or groups, like the ones found on the Internet to allow employees to discuss projects efficiently.

Using video chat on an intranet makes it possible to hold meetings with people in another office or even a different building.

Intranet Web sites are the same as Web sites found on the World Wide Web. People on the Internet cannot access Web pages on an intranet Web site.

Set Up

An intranet Web site is very easy to set up since most companies already have a network that connects computers to share information. To set up a Web site, you simply connect another computer, called a Web server, to the existing network to store the Web pages.

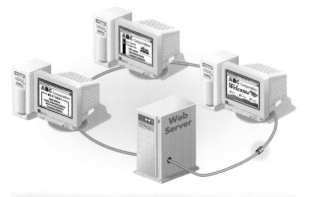

Compatibility

Intranets are very useful for companies that have different types of computers, such as IBM-compatible and Macintosh. Any computer that can run a Web browser can access the information available on an intranet Web site.

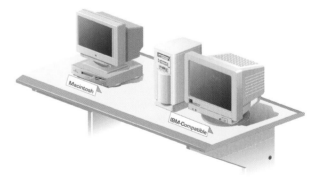

Employee Web Pages

If employees are connected to an intranet, they can easily publish their own Web pages.

Web pages can contain information such as office telephone numbers, current projects or any other information that might be important to fellow employees.

Department Web Pages

If a company has an intranet, any department in the company can display information on its own set of Web pages. A human resources department may display company policies and schedules.

A sales department might publish Web pages providing the latest sales figures.

Security

Many companies that have an intranet are also connected to the Internet. Most companies use a computer dedicated to maintaining security on the intranet to prevent people on the Internet from accessing information on the intranet.

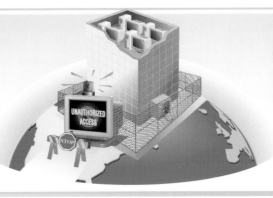

If someone tries to access the intranet from anywhere outside the intranet, the security computer will alert the network administrator.

INTRANET SOFTWARE

To set up an intranet, a company must have intranet software. There are many types of intranet software available.

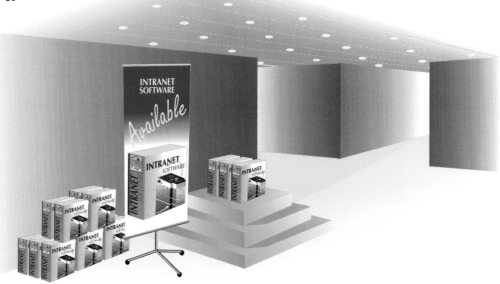

Intranet Suites

Most intranet software is available as a collection of several different applications sold together in one package, called a suite. Intranet suites usually consist of e-mail, Web publishing, database and security applications. When installing an intranet suite, you can decide which applications you want to use and install only those applications.

Networks

Intranet software is designed to be used by people connected to a company network. Most companies can turn a network into an intranet simply by adding a computer, called a server, to the network. Companies often add one server for each intranet application they want to use.

Netscape SuiteSpot

The company that created the Navigator Web browser also offers intranet software, called SuiteSpot. SuiteSpot is a collection of software that provides several intranet features.

You can get SuiteSpot at the following Web site:

http://www.netscape.com

Novell IntranetWare

Novell is well-known for its NetWare networking software and now also offers intranet software, called IntranetWare. IntranetWare offers many basic intranet features, but the main advantage of the suite is its compatibility with the Novell networking software.

You can find more information about IntranetWare at the following Web site:

http://www.novell.com/intranetware

Microsoft BackOffice

Microsoft now offers a set of intranet software, called BackOffice. BackOffice also includes an application called FrontPage that helps you easily organize and manage a large Web site.

You can find more information about BackOffice at the following Web site:

http://www.microsoft.com/backoffice

On an intranet, you can use the same types of applications that most organizations and companies use to perform tasks on a regular network.

HTML Conversion Features

To view the information in a document, you must often use the same application that created the document. To avoid this problem on an intranet, many applications now include a feature that makes it easy to convert a document into HTML (HyperText Markup Language). HTML is a computer language used to create Web pages. When information is converted into HTML, you can use any Web browser to view the information.

Project Management

Project management software helps you schedule meetings and keep track of resources used by people working on a project. By using the intranet to display project management information, every person involved in a project can instantly obtain information about the project.

Word Processors

Many word processors now help you easily convert documents into HTML. You can compose a document in a word processor and then quickly convert the document into a Web page. You can then display the page on the intranet Web site at your company or organization.

Spreadsheets

Converting information from spreadsheet programs into an intranet Web page allows you to distribute many types of useful information.

You can display sales figures or stock quotes for everyone in the company or organization to view.

Databases

Many companies use complex database programs to organize and store large collections of information.

Employees can use Web browsers and simple Web page forms to access information in a company database without having to learn how to use a complex database program.

Many companies that have intranets are also connected to the Internet. You must take precautions when connecting any computer or network to the Internet.

Firewalls

A firewall is software or a computer that restricts the information that passes between a private intranet and the Internet. Many companies use a firewall to prevent unauthorized individuals from accessing the intranet.

Access Restrictions

Some companies restrict people on the intranet from accessing certain parts of the Internet, such as chat or FTP sites. If a company restricts access to Web sites, employees will be able to view information on the intranet Web site, but they will not be able to view any sites on the World Wide Web.

Passwords

Some intranet services, such as newsgroups, require you to enter a login name and password to view information.

Login name:

Password:

Login names and passwords ensure that unauthorized employees do not have access to confidential company information.

Crackers

Crackers are people who like to test their skills by breaking into computer systems. Crackers usually do not try to break into intranets connected to the Internet.

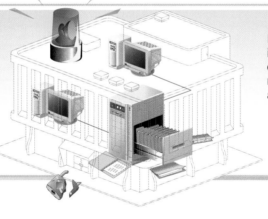

If crackers do break into your intranet, they will probably not cause any damage, but they may be able to view information available on the intranet.

Viruses

A virus is a program that disrupts the normal operation of a computer. A virus can cause a variety of problems, such as the appearance of annoying messages on the screen or the destruction of information on the hard drive.

Most companies constantly check for viruses on each computer connected to an intranet.

PGP

Pretty Good Privacy (PGP) is a security program you can use to ensure that no one else can read e-mail messages you send and receive.

Dear Ms. Mathur

I am highly interested in the Product Tester position recently advertised on the Internet.

I am attaching my resume and hope to hear from you soon.

FOR YOUR EYES ONLY

Private

Worlds Chat

Worlds Chat is a 3-D chat program that allows you to walk around and talk to other people in a three-dimensional world.

http://www.maran.com

URL

Each Web page has a unique address, called the Uniform Resource Locator (URL). You can instantly display any Web page if you know its URL.

Glossary

What is a phreaker? Is spamming encouraged on the Internet? What is the difference between cyberspace and meat space? Find out in this glossary.

2600

A loosely knit organization of hackers, crackers and phreakers. The number 2600 comes from the tone signal used to control telephone systems. This group can be found in the **alt.2600** newsgroup.

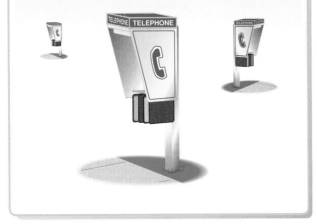

Appz

The term for application software, such as word processors and spreadsheet programs, that has been illegally copied and distributed over the Internet.

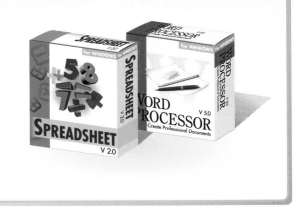

BBS

Bulletin Board System. BBSs are mostly used to allow people to exchange e-mail and access information. There are many BBSs available on the Internet.

Cache

An area of computer memory that stores recently used data. Cache makes browsing the Web faster by storing copies of Web pages you have recently viewed. When you want to view a Web page again, the browser retrieves the page from the cache instead of searching for the page on the Internet.

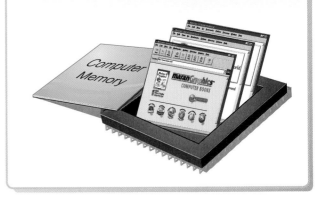

Camper

A type of character found in many multi-player games. Campers often hide in dark corners and shoot other players who pass by.

Cookie

Information used by a Web site to keep track of people who access the site. For example, when you visit a Web site, the site may create a cookie to store your name. The next time you visit the Web site, the site may display your name on the page.

Country Code

The part of an Internet address that indicates where the computer system that stores information is located. For example, "nl" in "company.com.nl" indicates that the computer system is located in the Netherlands. Internet addresses for the United States do not usually display a country code.

COUNTRY

au	Australia
ca	Canada
it	Italy
jp	Japan
uk	United Kingdom

Cracker

A person who breaks into computers and computer-controlled systems. Most crackers do not cause any damage. Crackers simply enjoy the challenge of breaking into computer systems.

Cyberspace

Another name for the Internet. When you browse the World Wide Web or send e-mail over the Internet, you are in cyberspace.

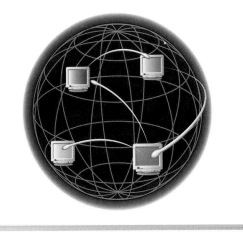

Daemon

A program that organizes and runs another program or system. An FTP daemon organizes and administers users who access an FTP site.

Dial-Up Connection

The type of connection to the Internet created by using a modem. Another type of connection is called dedicated. A dedicated connection is usually provided by a business or university and allows you to be continually connected to the Internet.

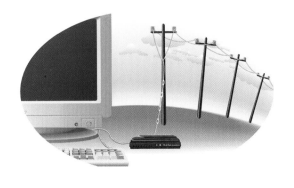

Digest

A collection of information. If you read a lot of messages from a mailing list or newsgroup, find out if the messages are available as a digest. A digest groups individual messages together and sends them to you as one message.

DNS Server

Domain Name System server. A computer that translates an Internet name such as "company.com" into a number such as 123.256.1.12. Computers and programs on the Internet need these numbers to understand where to send information. You must tell your computer what the name of your DNS server is before you can use the Internet.

EFF

Electronic Freedom Foundation. An organization whose mission is to protect the rights of the people who use the Internet.

Flame War

An argument where two or more people exchange angry or insulting messages. Usenet newsgroups are the most common place for flame wars to occur. Some flame wars involve hundreds of people and can last for months.

Flamer

A person who abuses other people in newsgroups or chat groups for almost any reason. Most flamers have short tempers and tend to react negatively when other people express different opinions.

Gamez

The term for games programs, such as flight simulators and electronic sports games, that have been illegally copied and distributed over the Internet.

Guru

A person who knows a lot about a specific topic. A person who is good at creating Web pages with HTML (HyperText Markup Language) is referred to as an HTML guru. Most gurus are willing to help beginners.

Hacker

A person who enjoys programming computers and making computers perform various tasks, such as controlling small appliances.

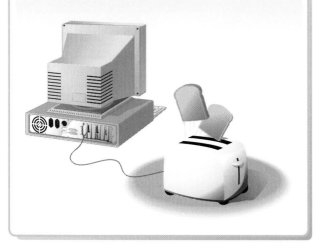

InterNIC

The organization responsible for distributing and organizing the names of all the networks on the Internet. If you want to set up your own Web site using a name you picked yourself, such as "www.abc.com", you have to apply to InterNIC to register the name.

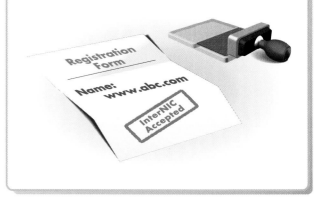

Lamer

A person who acts without thinking. Someone who posts a question to a newsgroup without first reading the FAQ for the newsgroup would be considered a lamer.

Llama

A newer Internet term referring to a person who complains about Internet-related problems. This term is commonly used in the multi-player game world.

Lurker

A person who joins a mailing list, newsgroup or chat session and does not participate. Lurking allows you to find out what the current topic of discussion is and see how people are communicating.

Mainframe

A powerful computer that can process and store large amounts of information and support many users at the same time. Mainframes are often used by large corporations and organizations.

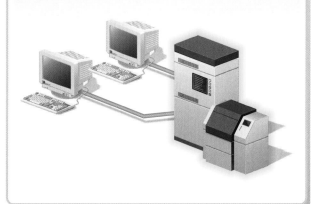

Meat Space

The real world we all live in. Meat space is the opposite of cyberspace.

MIME

Multi-purpose Internet Mail Extension. MIME allows you to attach programs, pictures and sounds to your e-mail messages and newsgroup articles. Most e-mail and newsgroup programs allow you to send and receive MIME attachments.

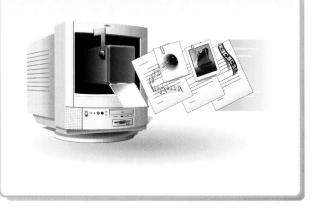

Mirror Site

A site that provides the same information as a popular site on the Internet. Mirror sites help reduce the amount of traffic on popular sites by giving people alternative locations they can use. FTP and World Wide Web sites are the most common types of mirror sites.

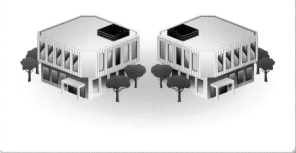

Mosaic

The first graphical World Wide Web browser for the Microsoft Windows operating system. Mosaic was developed by NCSA and made the Web much more popular and easy to use.

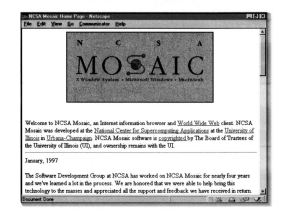

NCSA

National Center for Supercomputing Applications. NCSA created Mosaic, the first graphical Web browser. NCSA is located at the University of Illinois at Urbana-Champaign.

Net

Another name for the Internet. When you browse the World Wide Web or send e-mail over the Internet, you are on the Net.

Netizen

A "Citizen of the Internet." The term usually refers to a person who uses the Internet frequently.

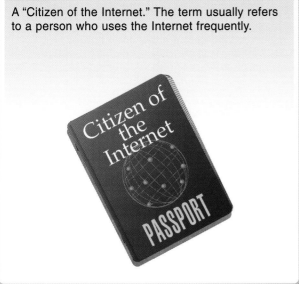

Newbie

A person who is new to the Internet. The Internet is so vast that newbies often get lost and need help from more experienced users. Newbie is generally considered a derogatory term.

PHREAKER TO TERMINAL

Phreaker

A specialist in telephone equipment and telephone companies. Phreakers may break into phone systems to make free long-distance calls, obtain calling card numbers or bug the neighbor's telephone.

Ping

A message your computer sends to another computer. A ping tells you whether the computer you are trying to contact is available on the Internet and how long the message takes to travel between the computers. The term comes from the navy, where submarines send a ping to find out if other submarines are around.

Puppy

A person who does something frequently. A person who collects a lot of Warez is referred to as a Warez Puppy.

RTFAQ

Read The FAQ. A FAQ (Frequently Asked Questions) is a document containing a list of questions and answers that often appear in a newsgroup. This comment is usually directed to people who ask questions in a newsgroup without first reading the FAQ.

Signature

A message that is usually no more than four lines long and is attached to the end of your e-mail messages and newsgroup articles. Signatures commonly contain your e-mail address, name, nickname and a quote.

Spam

Any advertising in an inappropriate location on the Internet. Posting sales information to a newsgroup that does not have an advertising theme is an example of spam. Spamming is strongly discouraged on the Internet.

SYN Attack

A process used by vandals to shut down a site on the World Wide Web. When a Web site is the subject of a SYN attack, no one can access the Web site.

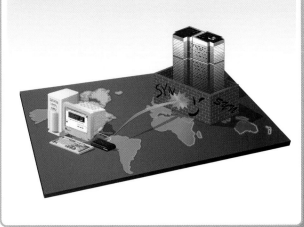

Terminal

A monitor and keyboard that are connected to a mainframe. Terminals can only display text and are simply used to input and output information.

TROLL TO WIZARD

Troll

A newsgroup article posted with the intention of starting a flame war. Trolls often make a statement that is obviously false and try to pass it off as the truth in the hope that someone will disagree.

Newsgroup:
rec.music.misc

I just saw Elvis at the 7-11 around the corner from my house!

Tube Time

The time spent using a computer. The tube refers to the picture tube in the monitor of a computer.

Unix

An operating system developed in the late 1960s. Most of the big computers on the Internet use the Unix operating system. You do not need to know any Unix commands to use the Internet.

VT100

A type of computer terminal that was used with old mainframe computers. When you use a telnet program to connect to a server on the Internet, the telnet program tricks the server into thinking your computer is a VT100 terminal.

Warez

A general term for software that has been illegally copied and distributed over the Internet. Most Warez can be found using IRC chat channels.

Warlording

The art of criticizing the signature at the bottom of e-mail messages and newsgroup articles. You can find examples of warlording in the **alt.fan.warlord** newsgroup.

Wirehead

A person who spends a lot of time using and working on computers. Most of their time is spent tinkering with the computer, as opposed to actually using the computer.

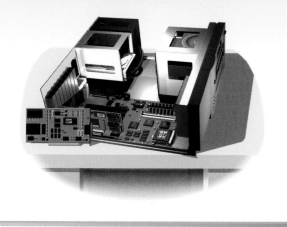

Wizard

A person who knows a lot about certain parts of the Internet. The term is most often found in the MUD (Multi-User Dungeon) community, where a wizard is the person who runs a MUD.

INDEX

INDEX

G

H

INDEX

I

images
- at FTP sites, 226
- on Web, 73, 105, 112-113

information on Internet, 6
- transfer explained, 14-15

Information Superhighway, 4. *See also* Internet

inline images, 112

Internet. *See also specific subject*
- catalogs on, 49
- chat. *See* chat
- connecting to, 20-21. *See also* connecting to Internet
- connection terms, 40-41
- databases on, 48
- directories on, 49
- education on, 50-51, 195
- future, 16-17
- history, 12-13
- information, 6-7, 46-47
  - free, providers of, 11
  - transfer explained, 14-15
- listings on, 49
- overview, 4-5
- payment for, 10-11
- service providers, 28-31
- television, 16
- users of, 8-9
- Web broadcasting, 52-53

Internet Explorer, Microsoft, 64-65.
  See also Web browsers

Internet Relay Chat. *See* IRC

InterNIC, 286

intranets
- applications, 276-277
- overview, 270-271
- security, 273, 278-279
- software, 274-275
- Web sites, 272-273

IP (Internet Protocol)
- addresses, 40
- numbers
  - Gopher, 248
  - telnet, 217

IRC (Internet Relay Chat)
- channels, examples, 208-209
- commands, 200-201
- etiquette, 202-203
- networks, 198
- overview, 196-197
- programs, 199, 200

ISDN (Integrated Services Digital Network), 25

ISPs (Internet Service Providers), 28-31

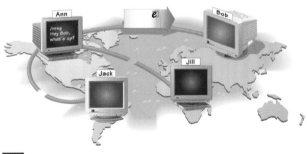

J

Java, 76-77

JavaScript, 78

JPEG (Joint Photographic Experts Group), 113.
  See also images

Jughead, 249

K

kill files, newsgroups, 171

L

lamers, 287

links in Web pages, 105, 110-111
- checking, 117, 119
- exchanging, 120

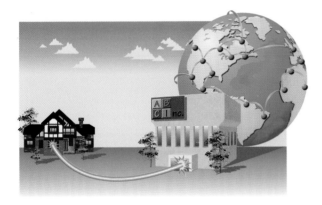

INDEX

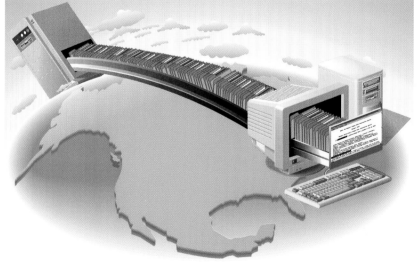